THE
NORTON SCORES

An Anthology for Listening

Third Edition • Expanded

Volume 1

THE

NORTON SCORES

An Anthology for Listening

THIRD EDITION • EXPANDED
IN TWO VOLUMES

VOLUME I:
GREGORIAN CHANT TO BEETHOVEN

EDITED BY

ROGER KAMIEN

ASSOCIATE PROFESSOR OF MUSIC, QUEENS COLLEGE
OF THE CITY UNIVERSITY OF NEW YORK

W · W · NORTON & COMPANY
New York · London

Acknowledgments

The score for item 3 is reprinted with the permission of Éditions de l'oiseau-lyre, Monaco.

The score for item 7 is reprinted from Josquin, *Wereldlijke Werken,* Deel II, Bundel V, edited by Antonowycz and Elders, with the permission of the Vereniging voor Nederlandse Muziekgeschiedenis.

The scores for item 9, from *Arcadelt Opera Omnia,* volume 2, edited by Albert Seay, and for item 13, from *Gabrieli Opera Omnia,* volume 2, edited by Denis Arnold, are reprinted here with the permission of Dr. Armen Carapetyan, General Editor of Corpus Mensurabilis Musicae and Director of the American Institute of Musicology.

The score for item 10 is reprinted from *Complete Works of Giovanni Pierluigi da Palestrina,* Vol. XXIX, pp. 77ff., edited by Lino Bianchi, and published by the Istituto Italiano per la Storia della Musica, with whose permission it is included here.

The score for item 14 is reprinted with the permission of Novello Publications, Inc.

The score for item 16 is reprinted with the permission of Galaxy Music Corporation.

The scores for items 22 (vocal selections), 28, and 32 are reprinted with the permission of G. Schirmer, Inc.

Library of Congress Cataloging in Publication Data
Kamien, Roger, comp.
    The Norton scores.
    Includes indexes.
    CONTENTS: v. 1. Gregorian chant to Beethoven.—
v. 2. Schubert to Davidovsky.
    1. Music—Analysis, appreciation. I. Title.
MT6.K22N7 1977b   780'.15   76-52467
ISBN 0-393-02197-1 (v. 1)
ISBN 0-393-09116-3 (v. 1) pbk.

4 5 6 7 8 9 0

Contents

Preface   *vii*

How to Follow the Highlighted Scores   *xi*

A Note on Performance Practice   *xi*

1. GREGORIAN CHANT, Introit, *Gaudeamus omes*   3
2. ANONYMOUS MOTET, *O miranda dei karitas—Salve mater salutifera—Kyrie*   5
3. GUILLAUME DE MACHAUT, Kyrie from *Messe de Notre Dame*   7
4. GUILLAUME DUFAY, *Alma redemptoris mater*   12
5. ANTOINE BUSNOIS, *Amour nous traicte—Je m'en vois*   18
6. JOSQUIN DES PREZ, *Déploration sur la mort de Johan Okeghem*   22
7. JOSQUIN, *Scaramella*   30
8. JOSQUIN, Agnus Dei from *Missa L'homme armé (sexti toni)*   32
9. JACOB ARCADELT, *Il bianco cigno*   46
10. GIOVANNI PIERLUIGI DA PALESTRINA, Sanctus from *Missa Ascendo ad Patrem*   49
11. ROLAND DE LASSUS, Introduction and first motet from *Prophetiae sibyllarum*   55
12. THOMAS MORLEY, *Sing We and Chant It*   60
13. GIOVANNI GABRIELI, *Nunc dimittis*   62
14. CLAUDIO MONTEVERDI, Scene from *L'Orfeo*   74
15. MONTEVERDI, *Zefiro torna*   79
16. THOMAS WEELKES, *As Vesta Was Descending*   89
17. HEINRICH SCHÜTZ, *Saul*   99
18. ARCANGELO CORELLI, *Trio Sonata*, Opus 4, No. 1   113
19. HENRY PURCELL, *Dido's Lament* from *Dido and Aeneas*   118
20. ANTONIO VIVALDI, *Concerto Grosso in D minor*, Opus 3, No. 11   121
21. GEORGE FRIDERIC HANDEL, *Piangerò* from *Giulio Cesare*   147
22. HANDEL, Excerpts from *Messiah*
     No. 1: Overture   *150*
     No. 2: *Comfort ye*   *154*

No. 3: *Ev'ry valley* 157
No. 12: *For unto us a Child is born* 163
No. 44: *Hallelujah* 174
23. JOHANN SEBASTIAN BACH, *Organ Fugue in G minor (Little)* 185
24. BACH, *Brandenburg Concerto No. 2 in F major* 190
25. BACH, Air and Gigue from *Suite No. 3 in D major* 226
26. BACH, *Cantata No. 140, Wachet auf* 234
27. DOMENICO SCARLATTI, *Sonata in C minor, K. 12* 289
28. CHRISTOPH WILLIBALD GLUCK, *Che farò senza Euridice?*
from *Orfeo ed Euridice* 291
29. JOSEPH HAYDN, *Symphony No. 94 in G major (Surprise)* 294
30. WOLFGANG AMADEUS MOZART, *Piano Concerto in C major, K. 467* 357
31. MOZART, *Eine kleine Nachtmusik* 451
32. MOZART, Excerpts from *Don Giovanni*
No. 1: Introduction 475
No. 4: *Catalogue Aria* 487
No. 7: Duet: *Là ci darem la mano* 495
33. MOZART, *Symphony in G Minor, K. 550* 500
34. LUDWIG VAN BEETHOVEN, First movement from *String Quartet in
F major*, Opus 18, No. 1 566
35. BEETHOVEN, *Piano Sonata in C minor*, Opus 13 *(Pathétique)* 578
36. BEETHOVEN, *Symphony No. 5 in C minor* 594

Appendix A. Reading an Orchestral Score 731
Appendix B. Instrument Names and Abbreviations 733
Appendix C. Glossary of Musical Terms Used in the Scores 738
Index of Forms and Genres 746

Preface

This anthology is designed for use in introductory music courses, where the ability to read music is not a prerequisite. The unique system of highlighting employed in this book enables students to follow full orchestral scores after about one hour of instruction. This system also has the advantage of permitting students who *can* read music to perceive every aspect of the score. It is felt that our system of highlighting will be of greater pedagogical value than artificially condensed scores, which restrict the student's vision to pre-selected elements of the music. The use of scores in introductory courses makes the student's listening experience more intense and meaningful, and permits the instructor to discuss music in greater depth.

The works included in this Third Edition have been chosen from among those most frequently studied in introductory courses. The selections range from Gregorian chant to the present day, and represent a wide variety of forms, genres, and performing media. In this Third Edition, increased emphasis has been placed on music of earlier periods and on music of the present century. A majority of the pieces are given in their entirety, while the others are represented by complete movements or sections particularly suitable for classroom study. Scenes from operas and some choral works are presented in vocal score, while all others are reprinted in their full original form. This anthology may be used independently, or along with any introductory text. The publishers have prepared a set of recordings to accompany *The Norton Scores.*

A few words about the highlighting system employed in the full scores: Each system of score is covered with a light gray screen, and the most prominent line in the music at any given point is spotlighted by a white band (see No. 1 in sample on page x). In cases where two or more simultaneous lines are equally prominent, they are each highlighted. When a musical line continues from one system or page to the next, the white highlighting band ends with a wedge shape at the right-hand margin, and its continuation begins with a reverse wedge shape (see No. 2 in sample). By following these white bands in sequence through the score, the listener will perceive the notes corresponding to the most audible lines. Naturally, the highlighting will not *always* correspond with the most prominent instruments in a specific recording, for performances differ in their emphasis of particular lines. In such cases, we have highlighted those parts that, in our opinion, *should* emerge most clearly. (There are occasional passages in complex twentieth-century works where no single line represents the musical continuity. In such passages we have drawn the listener's attention to the most audible musical events while endeavoring to keep the highlighting as simple as possible.) To facilitate the following of high-lighted scores, a narrow white band running the full width of the page has been placed between systems when there is more than one on a page.

It must be emphasized that we do not seek here to *analyze* melodic structure, contrapuntal texture, or any other aspect of the music. The highlighting may break off before the end of a phrase when the entrance of another part is more audible, and during long-held notes the attention will usually be drawn to more rhythmically active parts. The highlight-ing technique has been used primarily for instrumental music; in vocal works, the text printed under the music provides a firm guideline for the novice score-reader.

A few suggestions for the use of this anthology may be found useful:

1. The rudiments of musical notation should be introduced with a view to preparing the student to associate audible melodic contours with their written equivalents. It is more important for the beginning student to recognize rising and falling lines, and long and short notes, than to identify specific pitches or rhythms. It is helpful to explain the function of a tie, and the layout of a full score.

2. Before listening to a work, it is best for the student to familiarize himself with the names and abbreviations for instruments used in that particular score (a glossary of instrumental names and abbreviations will be found at the conclusion of the book). We have retained the Italian, German, French, and English names used in the scores reproduced in this anthology. This exposure to a wide range of terminology will prepare the student for later encounters with scores.

3. The student should be careful to notice whether there is more than one system on a page of score. He should be alerted for tempo changes, repeat signs, and *da capo* indications. Since performances often differ, it is helpful for the instructor to forewarn the class about the specific repeats made or not made in the recordings used for listening.

4. When a piece is very fast or difficult, it is helpful to listen once without a score.

5. It is best to begin with music that is relatively simple to follow: e.g. (in approximate order of difficulty) Schubert, *An Sylvia;* the second movement of Vivaldi's *Concerto Grosso in D minor,* Opus 3, No. 11; the

first and third movements of Mozart's *Eine kleine Nachtmusik;* the Air from Bach's *Suite No. 3 in D major;* and the second movement of Haydn's *Symphony No. 94 in G major (Surprise).*

6. Important thematic material and passages that are difficult to follow should be pointed out in advance and played either on the recording or at the piano. (We have found that rapid sections featuring two simultaneously highlighted instruments sometimes present difficulties for the students—e.g. Beethoven, *Symphony No. 5,* first movement, m. 65 ff., and Mozart, *Symphony No. 40,* first movement, m. 72 ff.)

We have attempted to keep the highlighted bands simple in shape while showing as much of the essential slurs and dynamic indication as possible. Occasionally, because of the layout of the original score, stray stems and slurs will intrude upon the white area and instrumental directions will be excluded from the highlighting. (Naturally, the beginning of a highlighted area will not always carry a dynamic or similar indication, as the indication may have occurred measures earlier when the instrument in question was not the most prominent.) As the student becomes more experienced in following the scores, he can be encouraged to direct his attention outside the highlighted areas, and with practice should eventually develop the skill to read conventional scores.

I should like to record here my great debt to the late Nathan Broder, who originated the system of highlighting employed here and whose advice and counsel were invaluable. My thanks go also to Mr. David Hamilton, and to Claire Brook and Hinda Keller Farber of W. W. Norton, for many helpful suggestions. I am most grateful to my wife, Anita, who worked with me on every aspect of the book. She is truly the co-editor of this anthology.

R.K.

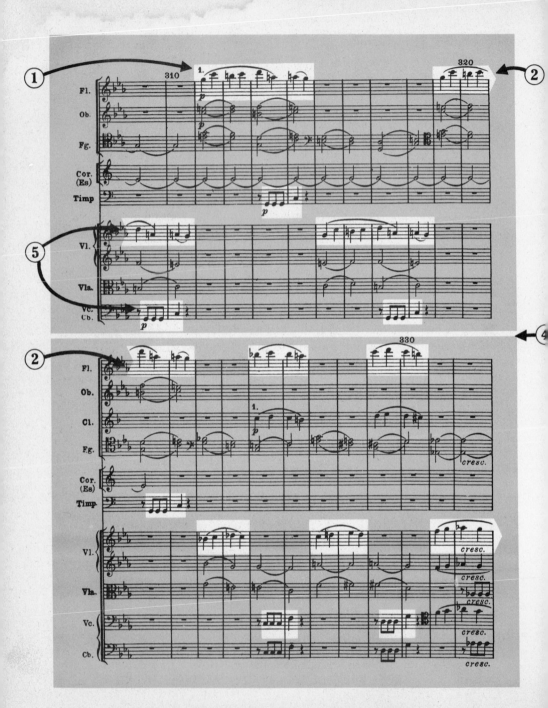

How to Follow the Highlighted Scores

1. The most prominent line in the music at any given time is high-lighted by a white band.

2. When a musical line continues from one system (group of staffs) or page to the next, the white highlighted band ends with a wedge shape, and its continuation begins with a reverse wedge shape.

3. By following the highlighted bands in sequence through the score, the listener will perceive the notes corresponding to the most audible lines.

4. A narrow white band running the full width of the page separates one system from another when there is more than one on a page. It is very important to be alert for these separating bands.

5. When two or more lines are equally prominent, they are each high-lighted. When encountering such passages for the first time, it is some-times best to focus on only one of the lines.

A Note on Performance Practice

In performances and recordings of earlier music, certain variations from the printed scores will frequently be observed. These are not arbitrary alterations of the music, but are based upon current knowledge concern-ing the performance practice of the period. In earlier times, the written notes often represented a kind of shorthand, an outline for performers, rather than a set of rigid instructions. The following specific practices may be noted:

1. Ornaments are frequently added to melodic lines, particularly at cadences and in repetitions of musical material.

2. During the Middle Ages and Renaissance, performers were often expected to supply sharps, flats, and naturals that were not written in the music. Some modern editors indicate these accidentals above the notes,

while others do not. Moreover, modern editors and performers often differ in their interpretation of the conventions governing the use of accidentals in early music.

3. In many early sources, the placement of words in relation to notes is not clearly indicated, or shown only in part; thus, modern editions and performances may differ.

4. In music before about 1600, the choice of voices or instruments and the choice of specific instruments was a matter of some freedom. Thus, in performance, some parts of a piece may be played rather than sung, or alternate between voices and instruments.

5. Since, at certain times and places in the past, pitch was higher or lower than it is today, modern performers sometimes transpose music to a key lower or higher than written, in order to avoid performance difficulties.

6. In Baroque music, the figured bass part, consisting of a bass line and numbers indicating harmonies, will be "realized" in different ways by different performers. In some editions included here (e.g. Monteverdi, *L'Orfeo*), a suggested realization is included by the modern editor—but it is only a suggestion, and will not necessarily be followed in a given performance.

THE
NORTON SCORES

An Anthology for Listening

Third Edition · Expanded

Volume 1

1. GREGORIAN CHANT, Introit, *Gaudeamus omnes*

In chant notation

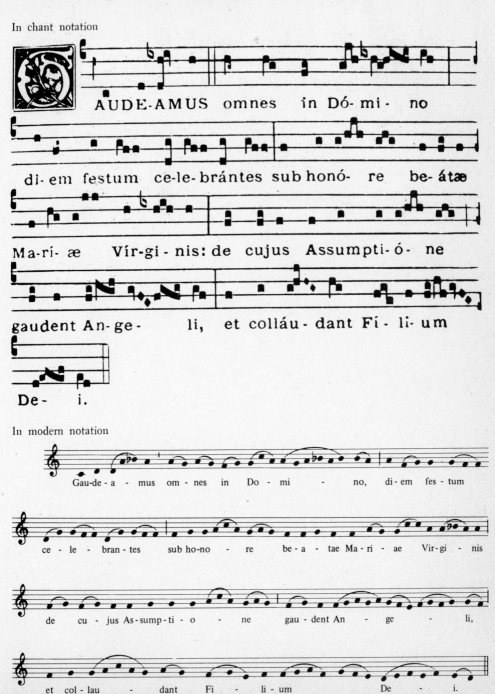

In modern notation

Translation

Gaudeamus omnes in Domino,	Let us all rejoice in the Lord,
diem festum celebrantes sub honore Mariae Virginis:	Celebrating a feast-day in honor of the Blessed Virgin Mary,
de cujus Assumptione gaudent Angeli,	For whose Assumption the angels rejoice
et collaudant Filium Dei.	And give praise to the Son of God.

2. ANONYMOUS MOTET, *O miranda dei karitas—Salve mater salutifera—Kyrie* (13TH CENTURY)

The Gregorian chant *Kyrie XII*, cantus firmus for the tenor

Translation

TRIPLUM

O miranda dei karitas!
Per peccatum cecidit
Homo quem condidit
Sed eius bonitas
Relaxavit penas debitas.
Adam mundum perdidit,
Sed vitam reddidit
Christi nativitas.

O wondrous love of God!
Through sin fell man
whom he made,
but His goodness
lightened the penalty owed.
Adam destroyed the world,
but life was restored to it
through the birth of Christ.

DUPLUM

Salve, mater salutifera,
Claritatis speculum,
Tu cordis oculum
Nostri considera,
peccatorum sana vulnera.
Virgo, salva seculum
A morte populum
eterna libera.

Hail, healing mother,
mirror of clarity,
consider the eye
of our heart,
heal the sinners' wounds.
Virgin, deliver the world
and free the people
from eternal death.

TENOR

Kyrie

3. GUILLAUME DE MACHAUT (c. 1300-1377), Kyrie from *Messe de Notre Dame* (c. 1364)

The Gregorian chant *Kyrie IV*, cantus firmus for the tenor

Translation

Kyrie eleison.	Lord, have mercy.
Christe eleison.	Christ, have mercy
Kyrie eleison.	Lord, have mercy.

4. GUILLAUME DUFAY (c. 1400-1474),
Alma redemptoris mater (c. 1495)

The chant *Alma redemptoris mater,* on which the top voice is based

to - rum _____ mi - se - re - re.

Translation

Alma redemptoris mater,	Gracious mother of the Redeemer,
quae pervia caeli porta manes,	Abiding at the doors of Heaven,
Et stella maris, succurre cadenti,	Star of the sea, aid the falling,
surgere qui curat populo.	Rescue the people who struggle.
Tu quae genuisti, natura mirante,	Thou who, astonishing nature,
tuum sanctum Genitorem,	Has borne thy holy Creator,
Virgo prius ac posterius,	Virgin before and after,
Gabrielis ab ore sumens illud Ave,	Who heard the Ave from the mouth of Gabriel,
peccatorum miserere.	Be merciful to sinners.

5. ANTOINE BUSNOIS (d. 1492), *Amour nous traicte—Je m'en vois*

Transcribed by Joshua Rifkin from Florence, Biblioteca Riccardiana, Ms. 2794, with corrections from Florence, Biblioteca nazionale centrale, Ms. Banco rari 229, and Paris, Bibliothèque nationale, Ms. f. fr. 15123. The transcription is a whole tone higher than and at half the note values of the manuscript sources.

- - - - - phe et de - - - bon -

sans vont di - sant Que g'y

Mes - di - sans vont di - sant

nai - - - - - - re.

vois pour Ma - ri - on, Ma - rion.

Que g'y vois pour Ma - ri - on, Ma - rion.

Translation

Amours nous traicte honnestement,	Love lures us guilelessly,
A josne nymphe et debonaire.	O young and comely nymph.
En bruit vers soy nottoirement,	With fanfare, and in full view,
Amours nous traicte honnestement.	Love lures us to him guilelessly.
Et desja tout bas vrayement,	And then ever so quietly,
Sans nombre offrant joyeulx sallaire,	Offering joyous rewards without limit,
Amours nous traicte honnestement,	Love lures us guilelessly,
A josne nymphe et debonaire.	O young and comely nymph.
Je m'en vois au vert bois	I am going to the green woods
Ouir chanter l'oisillon.	To hear the bird sing.
Mesdisans vont disant	Gossips are going to say
Que g'y vois pour Marion.	That I am going there for Marion.
Or y vont	Now shepherds and shepherdesses
Pastoreaux et pastorelles,	Go there
Et y font	And make
Ung touret et puis s'en vont.	A turn and then depart.
Je m'en vois au vert bois	I am going to the green woods
Ouir chanter l'oisillon.	To hear the bird sing.
Mesdisans vont disant	Gossips are going to say
Que g'y vois pour Marion	That I am going there for Marion.

6. JOSQUIN DES PREZ, (c. 1450-1521),
Déploration sur la mort de Johan Okeghem (c. 1495)

The chant from the Mass for the Dead on which the tenor is based

Translation

Nymphes des bois, déesses des fontaines,
 Chantres expers de toutes nations,
Changez voz voix fort clères et haultaines
 En cris tranchantz et lamentations,
Car d'Atropos les molestations
 Vostr'Okeghem par sa rigeur attrape,
Le vray trésoir de musicque et chief d'oeuvre,
 Qui de trépas désormais plus n'éschappe,
Dont grant doumaige est que la terre coeuvre.

Acoutrez vous d'abitz de deuil:
 Josquin, Brumel, Pierchon, Compère,
Et plorez grosses larmes d'oeil:
 Perdu avez vostre bon père.
Requiescat in pace. Amen.

TENOR
Requiem aeternam dona eis, Domine,
 et lux perpetua luceat eis.

Nymphs of the woods, goddesses of the streams,
 Fine singers of every nation,
Change your bright and lofty voices
 To piercing wails and lamentations.
For Atropos with cruel shears
 Your Ockeghem has taken,
Music's very treasure and true master
 From death can now no more escape,
And, great pity, in earth lies buried.

Clothe yourself in deepest mourning,
 Josquin, Brumel, Pierchon, Compère,
And from your eyes shed a flood of tears:
 For your good father now is lost.
May he rest in peace. Amen.

Eternal rest grant them, O Lord,
 And may your everlasting light shine on them.

7. JOSQUIN, *Scaramella* (PUBL. 1501)

Translation

Scaramella va alla guerra
 Colla lancia et la rotella,
La zombero boro borombetta,
La zombero boro borombo.

Scaramouche goes to war
With his lance and his shield,
With a rum-tum and a rum-tum-tum,
A rum-tum, rum-tum-tum.

Scaramella fa la gala
 Cholla scharpa et la stivala,
La zombero boro borombetta,
La zombero boro borombo.

Scaramouche plays the gallant
With his shoe and his boot,
With a rum-tum and a rum-tum-tum,
A rum-tum, rum-tum-tum.

8. JOSQUIN, Agnus Dei
from *Missa L'homme armé (sexti toni)* (PUBL. 1502)

The tune *L'homme armé*

In the Recordings for *The Norton Scores*, this is sung a tone higher.

Translation

Agnus Dei,
qui tollis peccata mundi,
miserere nobis,
dona nobis pacem.

Lamb of God,
Who takest away the sins of the world,
Have mercy upon us,
Grant us peace

9. JACOB ARCADELT (c. 1505-c. 1560),
Il bianco cigno (PUBL. 1539)

In the Recordings for *The Norton Scores*, this is sung a tone higher.

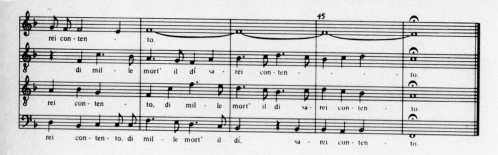

Translation

Il bianco e dolce cigno cantando more,
et io piangendo giung'al fin del viver mio;
stran'e diversa sorte, ch'ei morte sconsolato,
et io moro beato.

The sweet white swan dies singing,
While I weep as I reach my life's end.
How strange that he dies disconsolate
And I die happy.

Morte che nel morire,
m'empie di gioia tutt'e di desire;
se nel morir'altro dolor non sento,
di mille mort'il di sarei contento.

Weary to the point of death,
Drained of all joy and desire,
I meet death without sorrow,
Content to die a thousand deaths a day.

10. GIOVANNI PIERLUIGI DA PALESTRINA (c. 1525-1594), Sanctus from *Missa Ascendo ad Patrem* (PUBL. 1601)

Benedictus

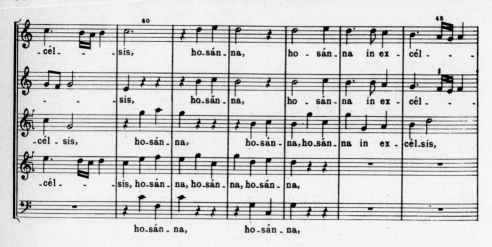

Translation

Sanctus, sanctus, sanctus,
Dominus Deus Sabaoth.
Pleni sunt coeli et terra gloria tua;
Hosanna in excelsis.
Benedictus qui venit in nomine Domini;

Hosanna in excelsis.

Holy, holy, holy,
Lord God of hosts.
Heavens and earth are full of thy glory;
Hosanna in the highest.
Blessed is he that cometh in the name of the
    Lord;
Hosanna in the highest.

11. ROLAND DE LASSUS (c. 1532-1594),
Introduction and first motet from *Prophetiae sibyllarum* (c. 1560)

Car - mi - na chro - ma - ti - ca, quae au - dis mo -

Car - mi - na chro - ma - ti - ca, quae au - dis mo -

Car - mi - na chro - ma - ti - ca, quae au - dis mo -

Car - mi - na chro - ma - ti - ca, quae au - dis mo -

du - la - ta te - no - re, Haec sunt il - la,

du - la - ta te - no - re, Haec sunt il - la,

du - la - ta te - no - re, Haec sunt il - la,

du - la - ta te - no - re, Haec sunt il - la, qui -

qui - bus nos-trae o - lim ar - ca - na sa-lu - tis Bis se -

qui - bus nos - trae o - lim ar - ca - na sa-lu - tis Bis se -

qui - bus nos-trae o - lim ar - ca - na sa - lu - tis Bis se -

bus nos-trae o - lim ar - ca - na sa - lu - tis Bis se -

Translation

Carmina chromatica,	Chromatic songs,

Carmina chromatica,
   quae audis modulata tenore,
Haec sunt illa,
   quibus nostrae olim arcana salutis
Bis senae intrepido,
   cecinerunt ore sibyllae.

SIBYLLA PERSICA

Virgine matre satus pando residebit aselli,

Jucundus princeps unus qui ferre salutem

Rite queat lapsis tamen illis forte diebus.
Multi multa ferent immensi fata laboris,
Solo sed satis est oracula prodere verbo:

Ille Deus casta nascetur virgine magnus.

Chromatic songs,
   which you hear in artful modulation,
These are the ones
   in which the secrets of our salvation
With bold voices, long ago,
   were sung by the twelve sibyls.

PERSIAN SIBYL

Born of a virgin, he will sit on the back of
   an ass.
The joyous prince who alone will bring
   happiness,
He the mighty one, in days to come.
Many will bear the heavy burden of labor,
Yet a single word is enough to utter the
   prophecy:
That great God will be born of a pure virgin.

12. THOMAS MORLEY (1557-1602),
Sing We and Chant It (PUBL. 1595)

13. GIOVANNI GABRIELI (1557-1612), *Nunc dimittis* (1615)

Translation

Nunc dimittis servum tuum, Domine,
Secundum verbum tuum in pace.
Quia viderunt oculi mei salutare tuum,
Quod parasti ante faciem omnium populorum,
Lumen ad revelationem gentium
et gloriam plebis tuae Israel.

Gloria Patri et Filio, et Spiritui Sancto:
Sicut erat in principio, et nunc et semper,
et in saecula saeculorum. Amen.

Now lettest Thou Thy servant depart, O Lord,
According to Thy Word, in peace.
For mine eyes have seen Thy salvation,
Which Thou hast prepared before all nations,
To be a light to illumine the Gentiles
And the glory of Thy people Israel.

Glory be to the Father, Son, and Holy Ghost:
As it was in the beginning, is now, and forever,
World without end. Amen.

14. CLAUDIO MONTEVERDI (1567-1643), Scene from *L'Orfeo* (1ST PERF. 1607)

e in - - te - ne - ri - to il cor___ del re de l'om - bre, me - co trar - rot - ti

a ri - ve - der le stel - le, o se ciò ne-ghe - ram-mi em - pio de - sti - no,

ri-mar-rò te - co, in com-pa-gnia di mor - te. Ad - dio ter - ra,

ad - dio cie - lo, e so - le, ad - di - - o.

365

365

Translation

ORFEO

Tu se' morta, se' morta, mia vita,
ed io respiro; tu se' da me partita,
se' da me partita per mai più,
mai più non tornare, ed io rimango—
no, no, che se i versi alcuna cosa ponno
n'andrò sicuro al più profondi abissi,
e intenerito il cor del re dell'ombre,

meco trarotti a riveder le stelle,
o se ciò negherammi empio destino,
rimarrò teco in compagnia di morte!
Addio terra, addio cielo, e sole, addio.

CORO DI NINFE E PASTORI

Ahi, caso acerbo, ahi, fat'empio e crudele,
ahi, stelle ingiuriose, ahi, cielo avaro.
Non si fidi uom mortale di ben caduco e frale,

che tosto fugge, e spesso a gran salita il
precipizio è presso.

You are dead, dead, my darling,
And I live; you have left me,
Left me forevermore,
Never to return, yet I remain—
No, no, if verses have any power,
I shall go boldly to the deepest abysses,
And having softened the heart of the king of
shadows,
Will take you with me to see again the stars,
Or if cruel fate will deny me this,
I will remain with you in the presence of death!
Farewell earth, farewell sky, and sun, farewell.

CHORUS OF NYMPHS AND SHEPHERDS

Ah, bitter chance, ah, fate wicked and cruel,
Ah, stars of ill omen, ah, heaven avaricious.
Let not mortal man trust good, short-lived and
frail,
Which soon disappears, for often to a bold
ascent the precipice is near.

15. MONTEVERDI, *Zefiro torna* (PUBL. 1632)

Translation

Zefiro torna e di soavi accenti
L'aer fa grato e'l piè discioglie a l'onde,
E mormorando tra le verdi fronde,
Fa danzar al bel suon su'l prato i fiori;

Inghirlandato il crin Fillide e Clori,
Note temprando amor care e gioconde;
E da monti e da valli ime e profonde,
Raddoppian l'armonia gli antri canori.

Sorge più vaga in ciel l'aurora el Sole,
Sparge più luci d'or più puro argento,
Fregia di Teti più il bel ceruleo manto.

Sol io per selve abbandonate e sole,
L'ardor di due begli occhi el mio tormento,
Come vuol mia ventura hor piango, hor canto.

The West Wind returns and with gentle accents
Makes the air pleasant and quickens one's step,
And, murmuring among the green branches,
Makes the meadow flowers dance to its lovely
sound.

With garlands in their hair Phyllis and Clorinda
Are sweet and joyous while Love makes music,
And from the mountains and valleys hidden
deep,
The echoing caves redouble the harmony.

At dawn the sun rises in the sky more gracefully,
Spreads abroad more golden rays, a purer silver,
Adorns the sea with an even lovelier blue mantle.

Only I am abandoned and alone in the forest,
The ardor of two beautiful eyes is my torment:
As my fate may decree, now I weep, now I sing.

16. THOMAS WEELKES (c. 1575-1623),
As Vesta Was Descending (PUBL. 1601)

17. HEINRICH SCHÜTZ (1585-1672), *Saul* (PUBL. 1650)

schwer wer - den, wi - der den Sta - chel zu lö - - cken.

Es wird dir schwer wer - den, wi - der den Sta - chel zu lö - - cken.

Translation

Saul, Saul, was verfolgst du mich? Es wird dir
schwer werden, wider den Stachel zu löcken.

Saul, Saul, why do you persecute me? It
will be hard for you to kick against the traces.

18. ARCANGELO CORELLI (1653-1713),
Trio Sonata, Opus 4, No. 1 (PUBL. 1694)

Preludio

Corrente

19. HENRY PURCELL (c. 1659-1695),
Dido's Lament from *Dido and Aeneas* (1ST PERF. 1689)

Thy hand, Bel - in - da! dark — — ness shades me, On thy

bos - om let me rest, More I would, but death— in -

vades me Death is now— a wel - come guest!

When I am laid,— am laid———— in

mem-ber me, but ah!_____ for - get my__ fate. Re-mem-ber me,

re - mem-ber me, But ah!_____ for-get my fate, Re-

mem-ber me, but ah!_____ for - get my__ fate.

20. ANTONIO VIVALDI (1678-1741),
Concerto Grosso in D minor, Opus 3, No. 11 (PUBL. 1712)

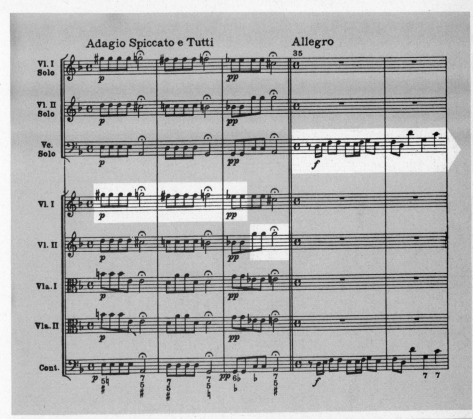

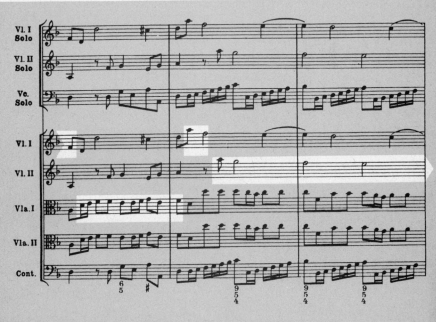

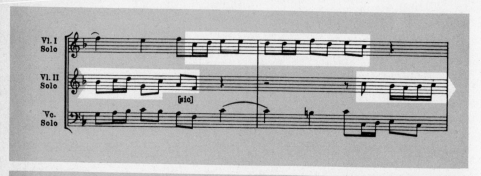

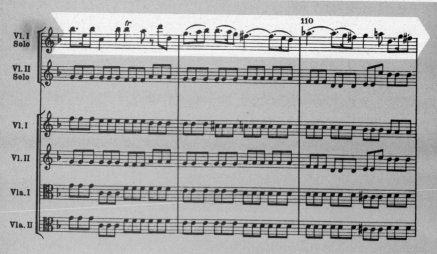

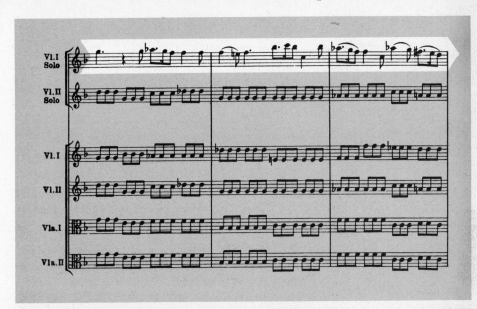

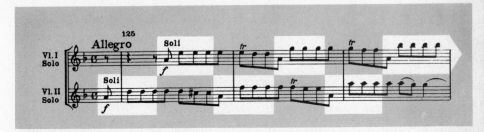

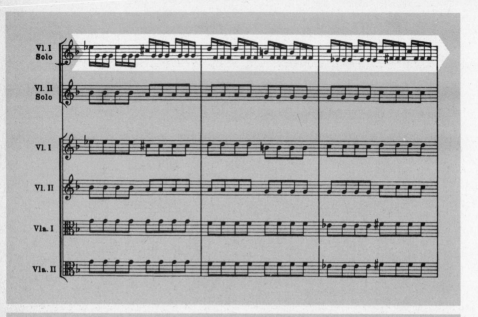

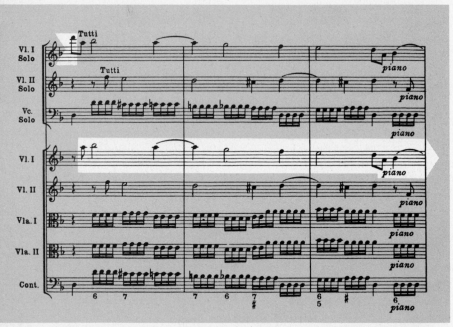

21. GEORGE FRIDERIC HANDEL (1685-1759),
Piangerò from Giulio Cesare (1ST PERF. 1724)

(Fine.)

Translation

Piangerò la sorte mia,
sì crudelo e tanto ria,
finchè vita in petto avrò.

Mà poi morte d'ogn'intorno
il tiranno e notte e giorno
fatta spettro agiterò.

I shall lament my fate,
so cruel and so wicked,
as long as there is life in my breast.

But when I am dead, from every side,
both night and day,
I, become a specter, will torment the tyrant.

22. HANDEL, Excerpts from *Messiah* (1741)

No. 1: Overture

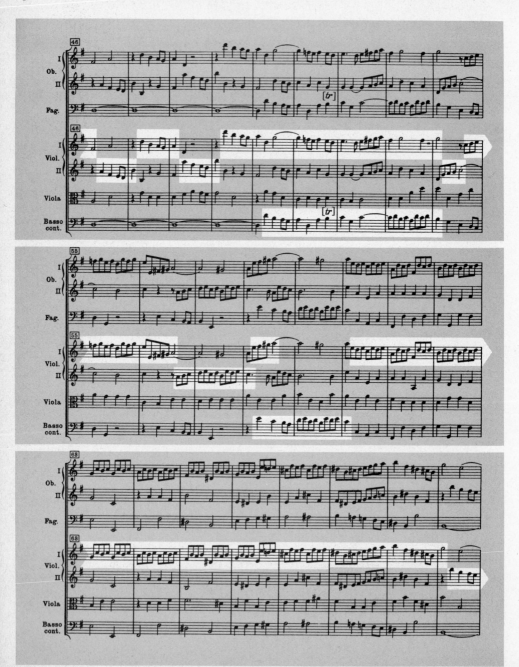

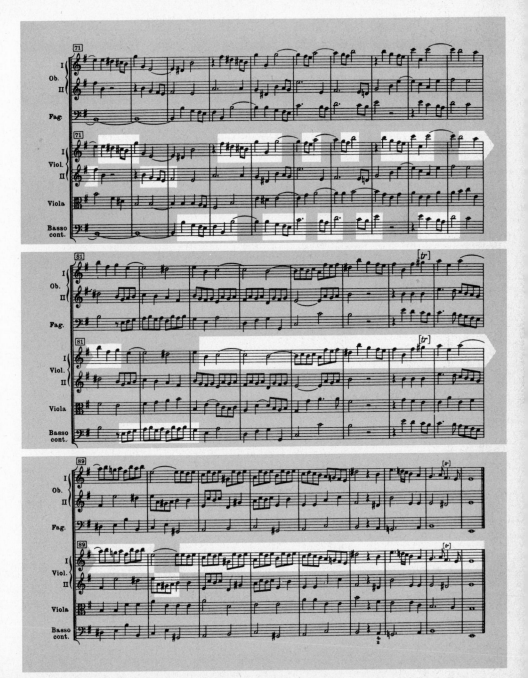

No. 2: *Comfort ye*

i - qui -ty is par-don'd, that her in - i - qui -ty is par - -

don'd.

mf

The voice of him that crieth in the wilderness, Pre-pare ye the way of the

Lord, make straight in the desert a high-way for our God.

No. 3: *Ev'ry valley*

No. 12: *For unto us a Child is born*

No. 44: *Hallelujah*

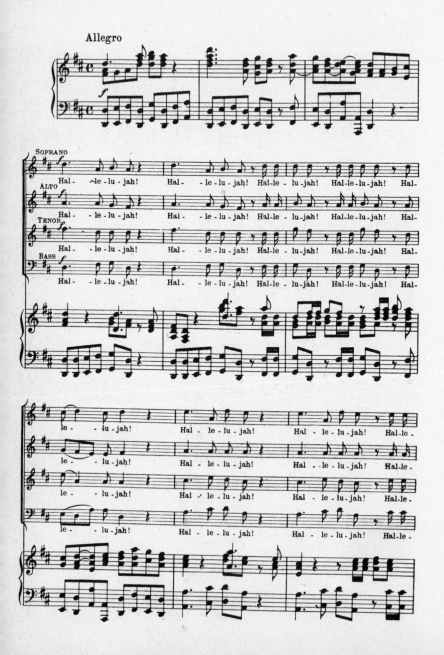

23. JOHANN SEBASTIAN BACH (1685-1750),
Organ Fugue in G minor (Little) (1709?)

Manual.

Pedal.

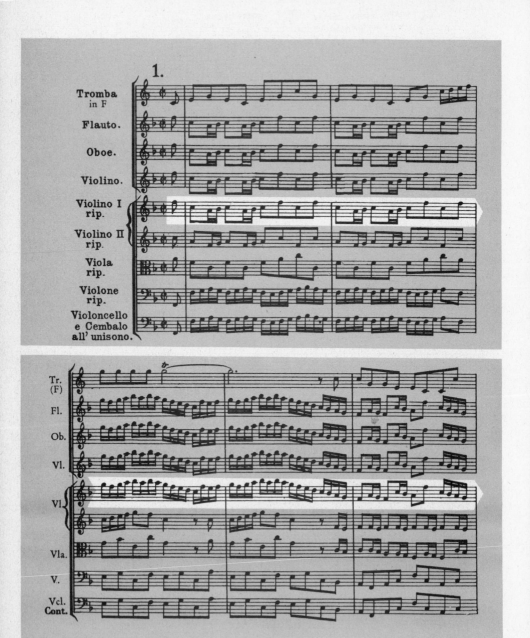

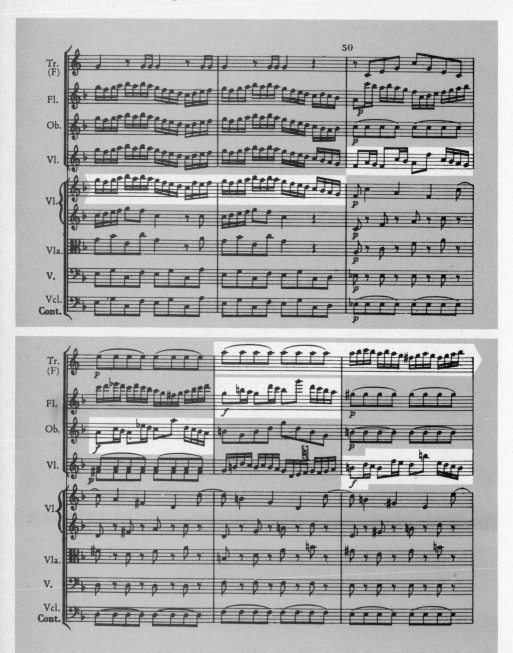

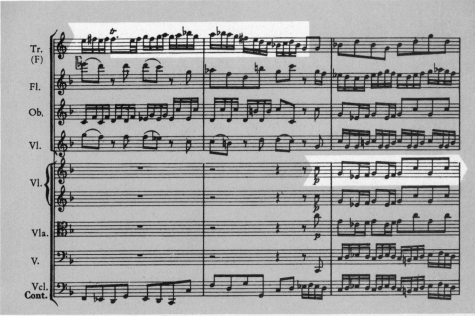

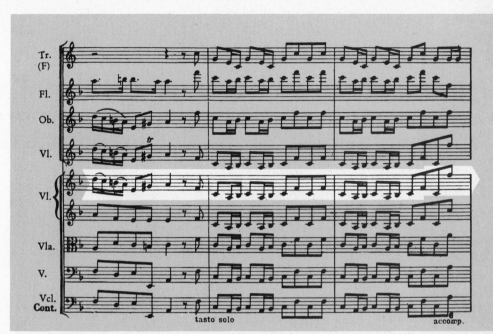

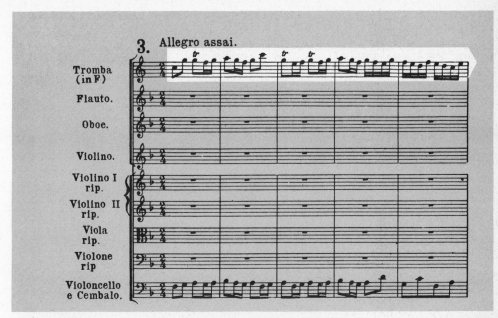

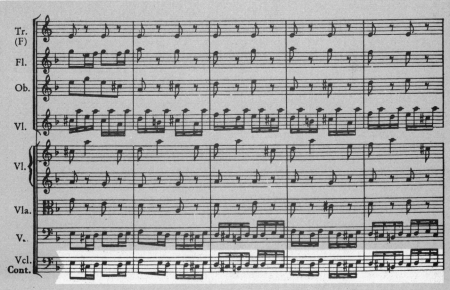

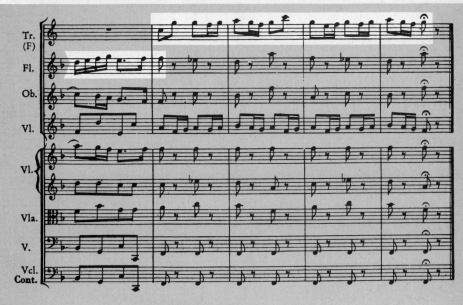

25. BACH, Air and Gigue from *Suite No. 3 in D major* (1723?)

26. BACH, *Cantata No. 140, Wachet auf* (1731)

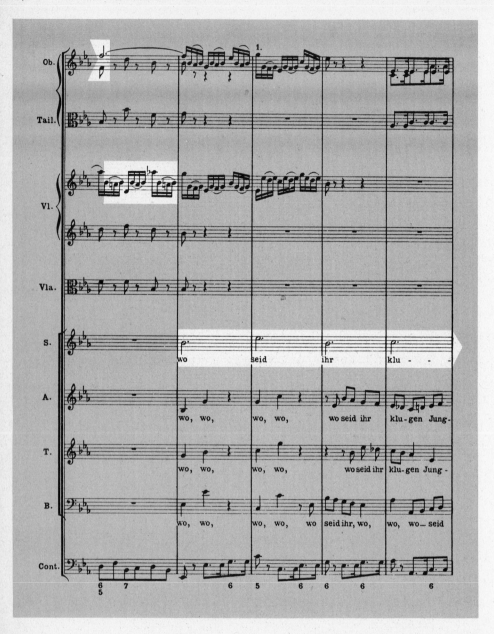

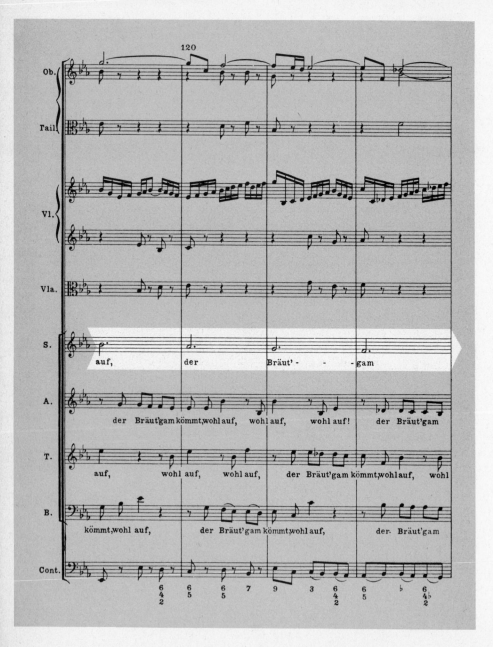

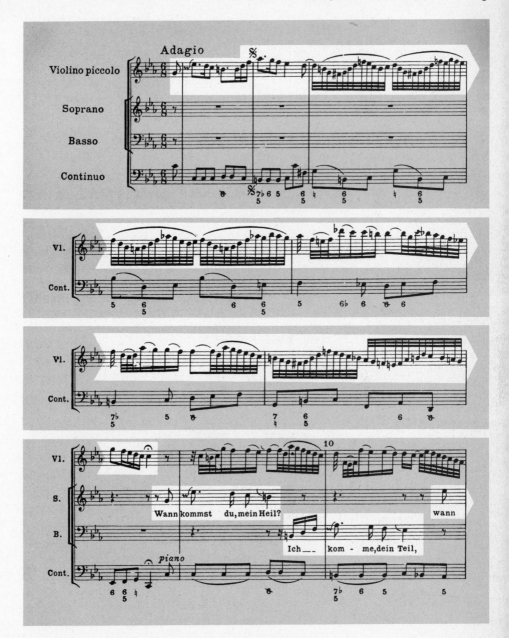

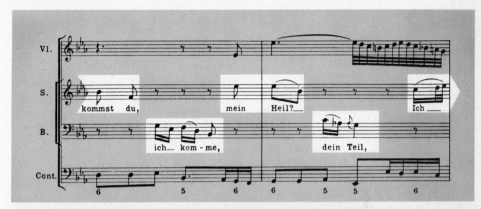

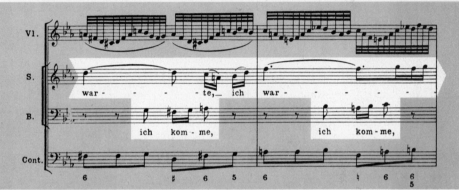

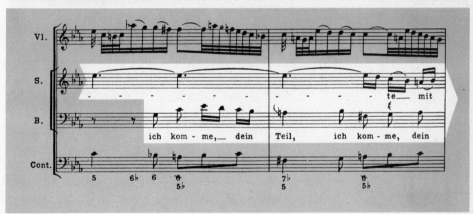

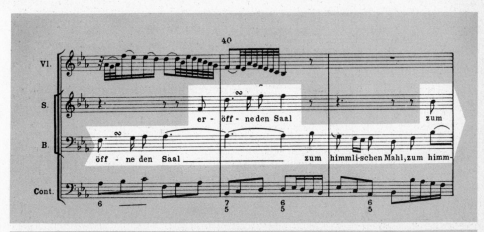

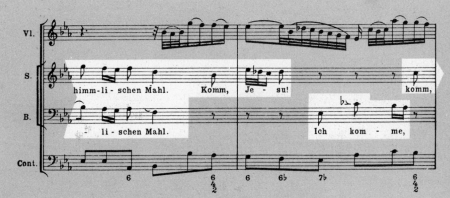

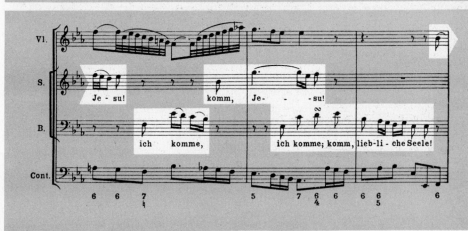

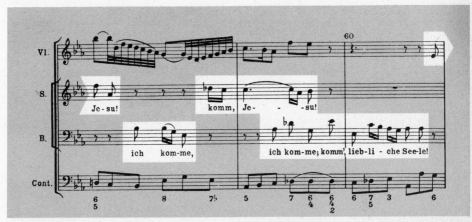

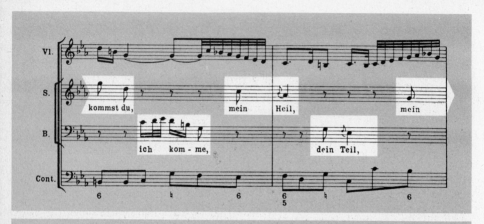

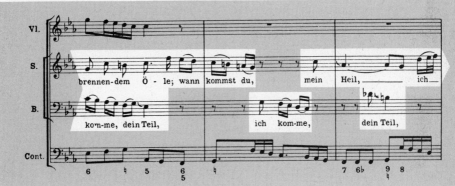

Dal Segno

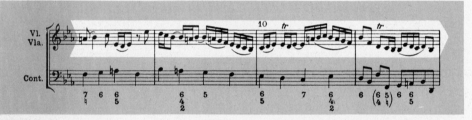

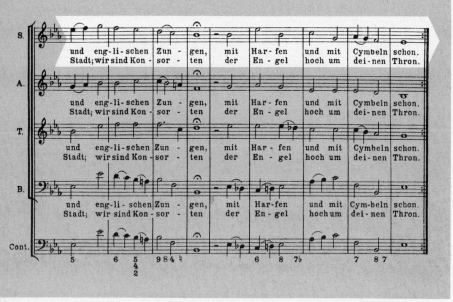

Translation

I

Wachet auf, ruft uns die Stimme
der Wächter sehr hoch auf der Zinne,
wach auf, du Stadt Jerusalem!

Mitternacht heisst diese Stunde;
sie rufen uns mit hellem Munde:
wo seid ihr klugen Jungfrauen?

Wohl auf, der Bräut'gam kömmt,
steht auf, die Lampen nehmt!
Alleluja!
Macht euch bereit zu der Hochzeit,
ihr müsset ihm entgegen gehn.

"Awake," the voice of watchmen
calls us from high on the tower,
"Awake, you city of Jerusalem!"

Midnight is this very hour;
they call to us with bright voices:
"Where are you, wise virgins?"

Take cheer, the Bridegroom comes,
arise, take up your lamps!
Hallelujah!
Prepare yourselves for the wedding,
you must go forth to meet him.

II

Er kommt, er kommt, der Bräut'gam kommt!
Ihr Töchter Zions, kommt heraus,
sein Ausgang eilet aus der Höhe
in euer Mutter Haus.

Der Bräut'gam kommt, der einem Rehe
und jungem Hirsche
gleich auf denen Hügeln springt
und euch das Mahl der Hochzeit bringt.

Wacht auf, ermuntert euch!
den Bräut'gam zu empfangen;
dort, sehet, kommt er hergegangen.

He comes, he comes, the Bridegroom comes!
Daughters of Zion, come forth,
he is hurrying from on high
into your mother's house.

The Bridegroom comes, who like a roe
and a young hart
leaping upon the hills
brings you the wedding meal.

Wake up, bestir yourselves
to receive the Bridegroom;
there, look, he come along.

III

Wann kommst du, mein Heil?
Ich komme, dein Teil.
Ich warte mit brennendem Öle;
Eröffne den Saal
zum himmlischen Mahl.
Ich öffne den Saal
zum himmlischen Mahl.
Komm Jesu!
      komm, liebliche Seele!

Soul: When will you come, my salvation?
Jesus: I am coming, your own.
Soul: I am waiting with burning oil.
      Throw open the hall
      to the heavenly banquet!
Jesus: I open the hall
      to the heavenly banquet.
Soul: Come, Jesus!
Jesus: Come, lovely Soul!

IV

Zion hört die Wächter singen,
das Herz tut ihr vor Freuden springen,
sie wachet und steht eilend auf.

Zion hears the watchmen singing,
for joy her very heart is springing,
she wakes and rises hastily.

Ihr Freund kommt von Himmel prächtig,	From heaven comes her friend resplendent,
von Gnaden stark, von Wahrheit mächtig,	sturdy in grace, mighty in truth,
Ihr Licht wird hell, ihr Stern geht auf.	her light shines bright, her star ascends.

Nun komm, du werte Kron,	Now come, you worthy crown,
Herr Jesu Gottes Sohn.	Lord Jesus, God's own Son,
Hosianna!	Hosanna!
Wir folgen all'	We all follow
zum Freudensaal	to the joyful hall
und halten mit das Abendmahl.	and share the Lord's Supper.

V

So geh herein zu mir,	Come enter in with me,
du mir erwählte Braut!	my chosen bride!
Ich habe mich mit dir	I have pledged my troth
in Ewigkeit vertraut.	to you in eternity!
Dich will ich auf mein Herz,	I will set you as a seal upon my heart,
auf meinen Arm	and as a seal upon my arm
gleich wie ein Siegel setzen,	and restore delight to your sorrowful eye.
und dein betrübtes Aug' ergötzen.	Forget now, o soul,
Vergiss, o Seele,	the anguish, the pain,
nun die Angst, den Schmerz,	which you had to suffer;
den du erdulden müssen;	on my left you shall rest,
auf meiner Linken sollst du ruh'n,	and my right shall kiss you.
und meine Rechte soll dich küssen.	

V I

Mein Freund ist mein!	Soul: My friend is mine!
Und ich bin dein!	Jesus: and I am his!
Die Liebe soll nichts scheiden.	Both: Love shall separate nothing!
Ich will mit dir in Himmels Rosen weiden,	Soul: I will feed with you among heaven's roses,
Du sollst mit mir in Himmels Rosen weiden,	Jesus: You shall feed with me among heaven's roses,
da Freunde die Fülle, da Wonne wird sein!	Both: There fullness of joy, there rapture shall be!

V I I

Gloria sei dir gesungen	Gloria be sung to you
mit Menschen-und englischen Zungen,	with men's and angels' tongues,
mit Harfen und mit Cymbeln schon.	with harps and beautiful cymbals.

Von zwölf Perlen sind die Pforten	Of twelve pearls are the gates
an deiner Stadt; wir sind Konsorten	at your city; we are consorts
der Engel hoch um deinen Thron.	of the angels high about your throne.

Kein Aug' hat je gespürt,	No eye has ever sensed,
kein Ohr hat je gehört	no ear has ever heard
solche Freude.	such a delight.
Des sind wir froh,	Of this we rejoice,
io, io!	io, io,
ewig in dulci jubilo.	forever *in dulci jubilo*.

MOVEMENTS 1, 4, AND 7 BY PHILIP NICOLAI;
MOVEMENTS 2, 3, 5, AND 6 ANONYMOUS.

TRANSLATED BY
GERHARD HERZ

27. DOMENICO SCARLATTI (1685-1757),
Sonata in C minor, Kirkpatrick 11 (PUBL. 1738)

28. CHRISTOPH WILLIBALD GLUCK (1714-1787),
Che farò senza Euridice? from *Orfeo ed Euridice* (1762, rev. 1774)

29. JOSEPH HAYDN (1732-1809), Symphony No. 94 in G major (Surprise) (1791)

I

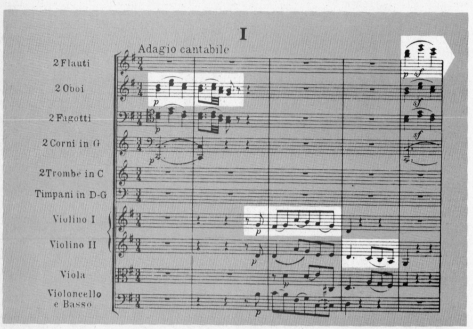

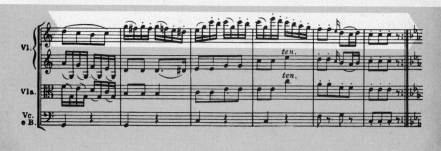

III

Menuetto Allegro molto

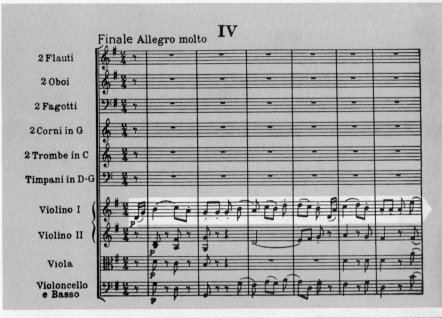

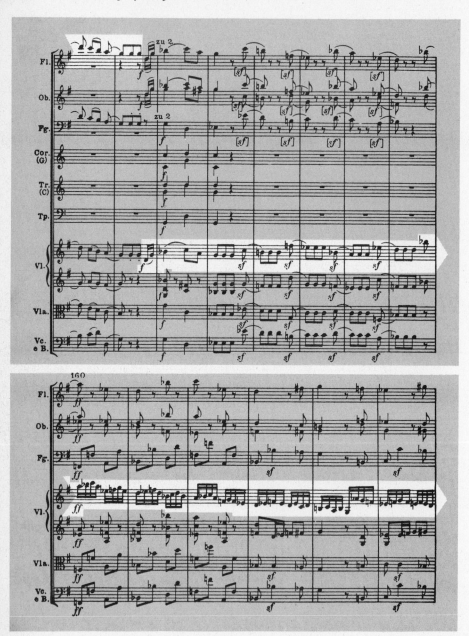

30. WOLFGANG AMADEUS MOZART (1756-1791),
Piano Concerto in C major, K. 467 (1785)

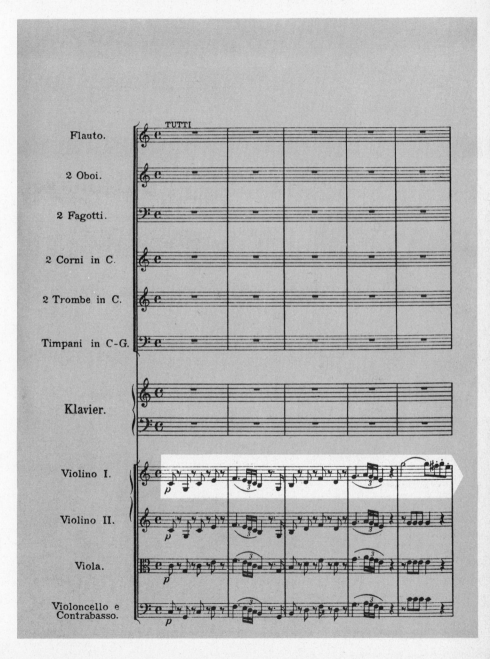

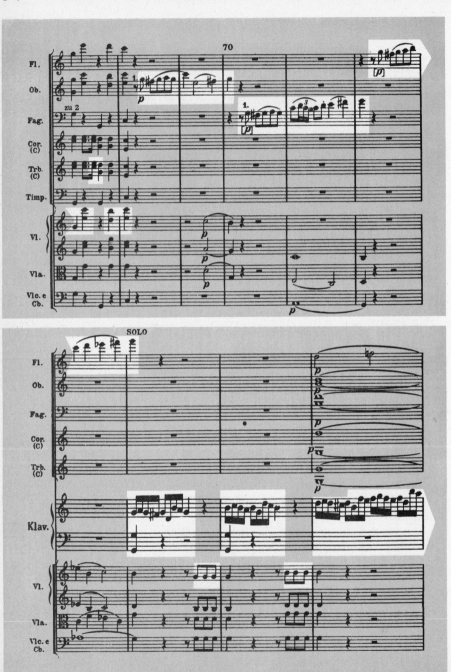

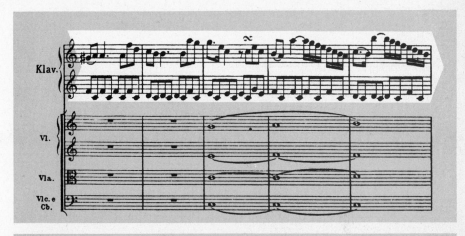

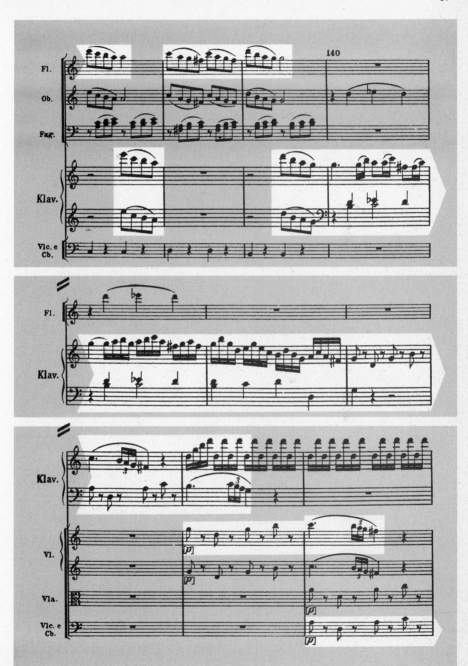

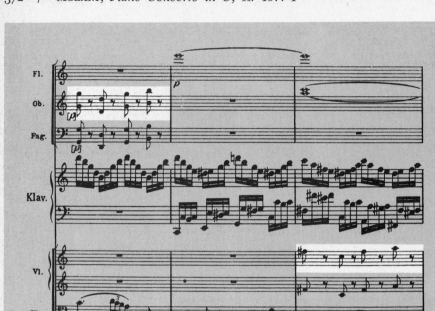

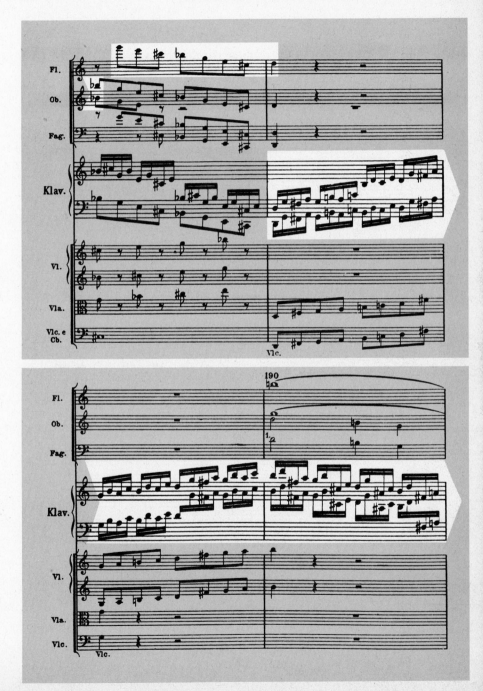

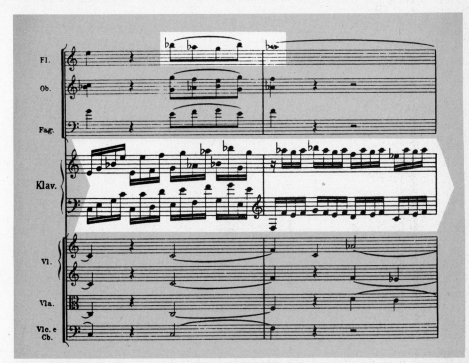

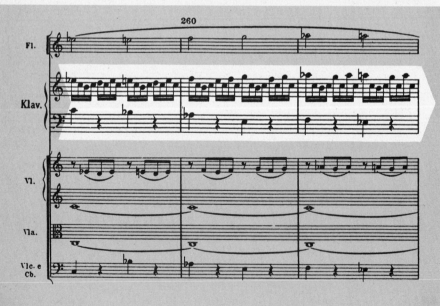

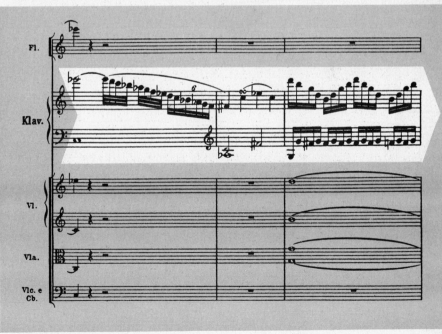

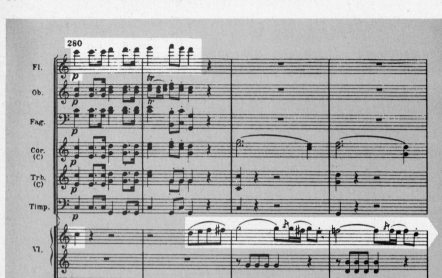

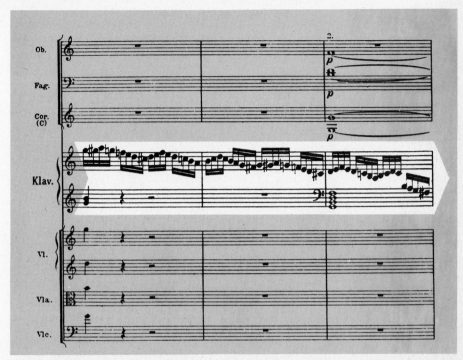

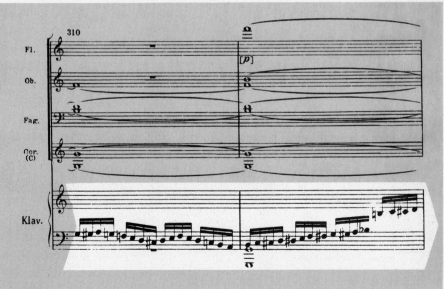

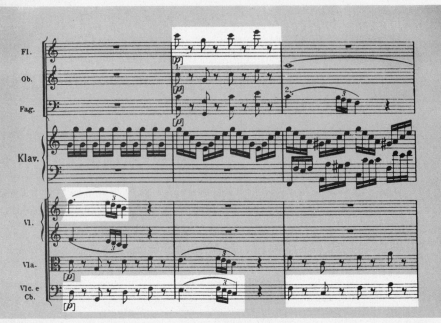

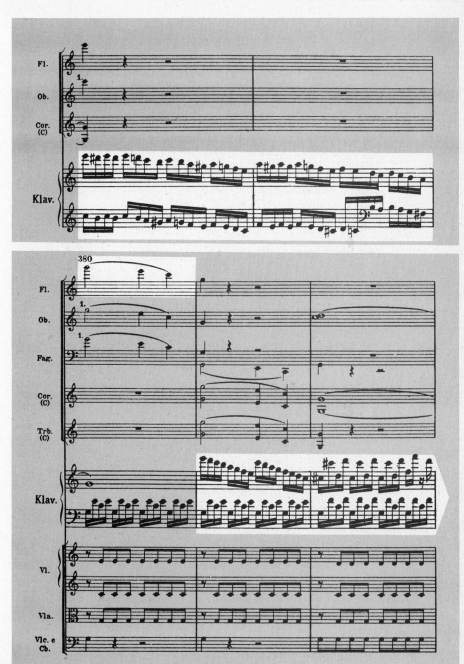

* Mozart did not leave written-out cadenzas for this concerto. Modern pianists supply their own or choose from among various published cadenzas.

II.

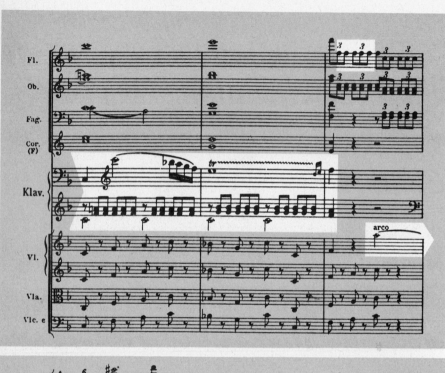

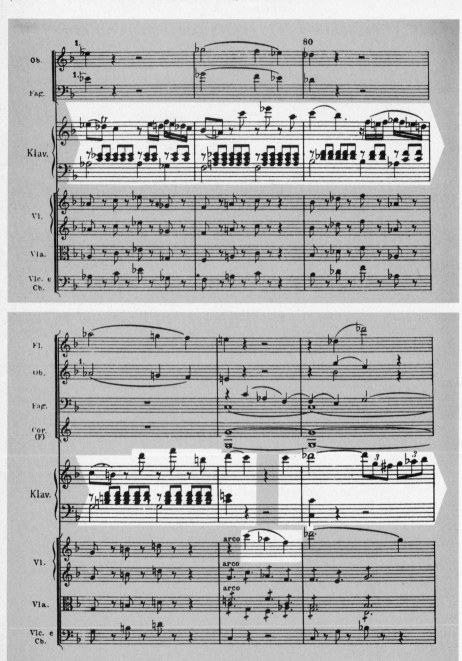

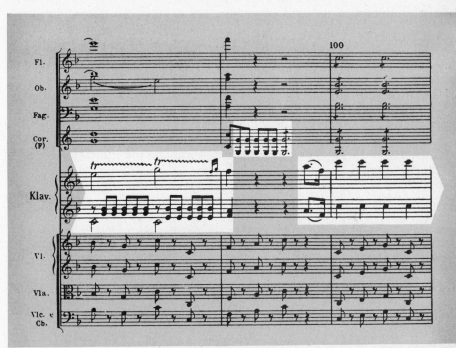

III.

Allegro vivace assai.

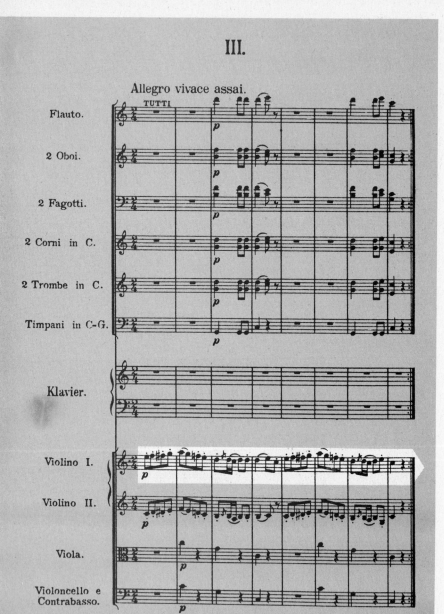

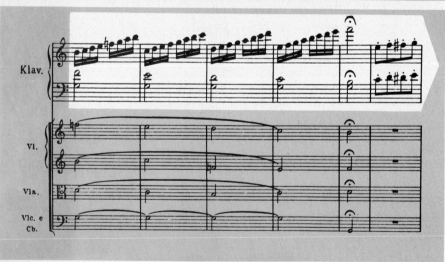

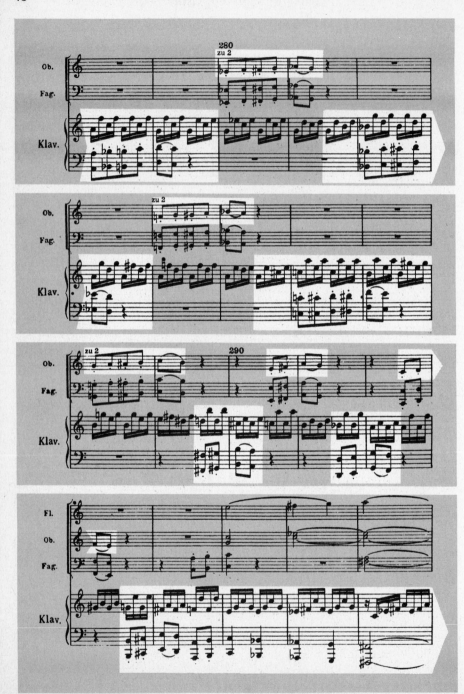

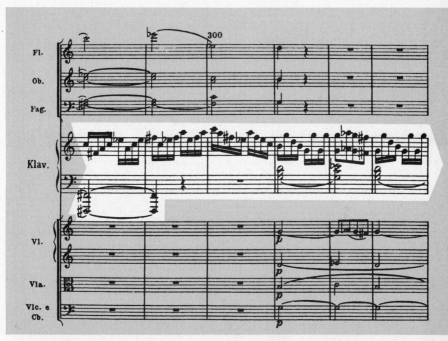

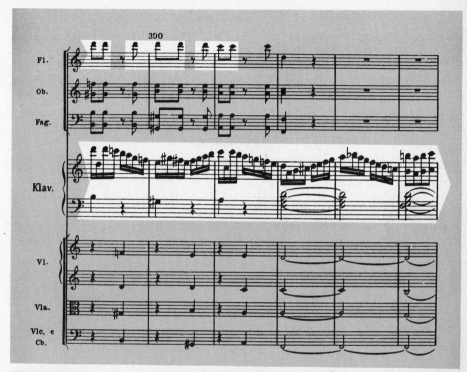

* See note on p. 405.

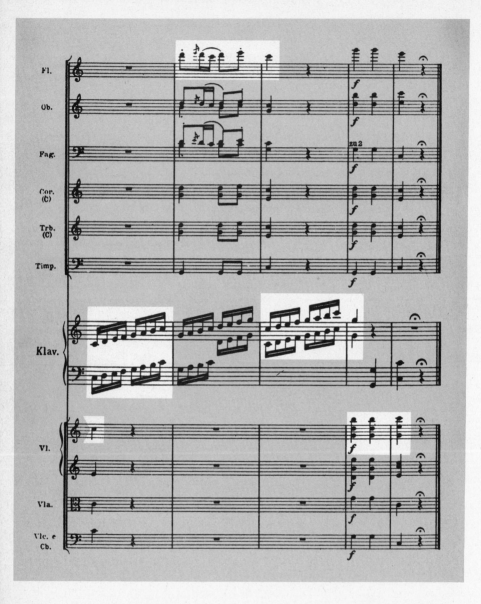

31. MOZART, *Eine kleine Nachtmusik* (1787)

II

Romanze
Andante

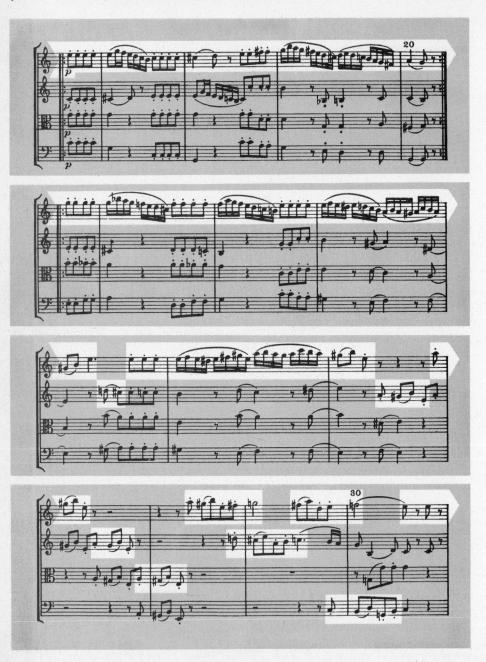

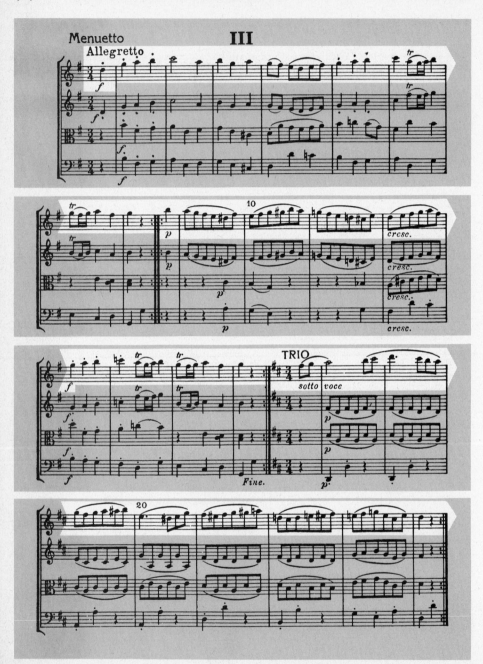

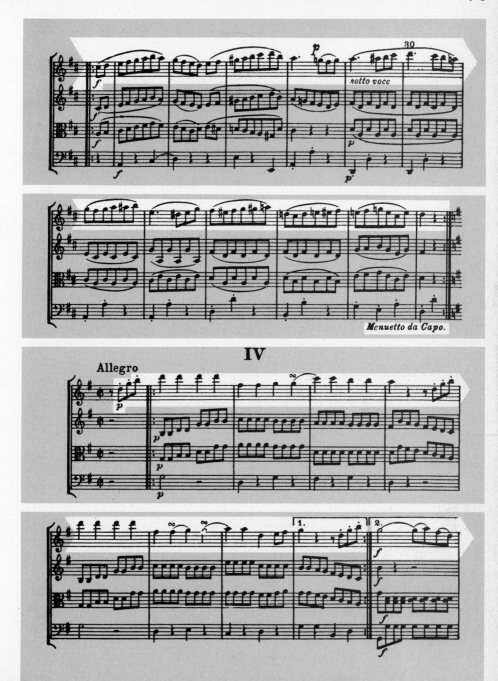

Menuetto da Capo.

IV

Allegro

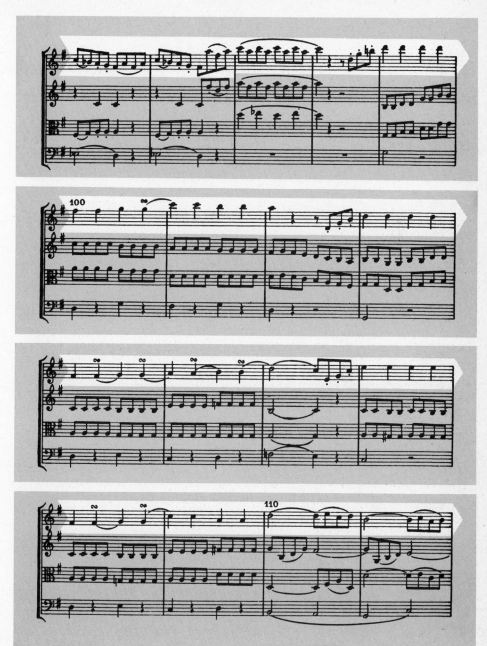

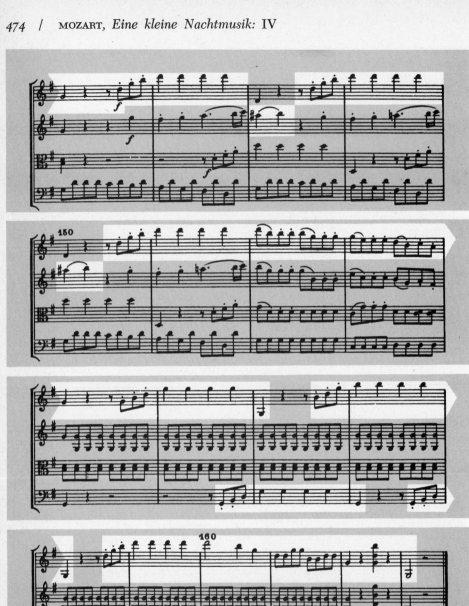

32. MOZART, Excerpts from *Don Giovanni* (1787)

No. 1: Introduction

Scene — A Garden, Night.

Leporello, in a cloak, discovered watching before the house of Donna Anna; then Donna Anna and Don Giovanni, afterwards the Commandant.

(wrapt in a dark mantle, impatiently pacing to and fro before the steps to the palace).

Leporello.

Not-te e gior-no fa-ti-car, per chi nul-la sa gra-dir; pio-va e
On the go from morn till night, Run-ning er-rands, nev-er free, Hard-ly

ven-to sop-por-tar, mangiar ma-le e mal dor-mir!
time to snatch a bite; This is not the life for me.

Vo - glio far il gen-til-uo-mo, e non
I would like to play the mas-ter, Would no

(Servants return with Don Octavio, and hasten with him from the street into the palace)

No. 4: *Catalogue Aria*

Ma-da-mi-na!
At your pleasure,

Il ca-ta-lo-go è
you may have a pe-

ques-to, del-le bel-le, che a-mo il padron mi-o; un ca-ta-lo-go è
rus-al Of the list that I keep for my mas-ter; But per-haps you'll di-

gli è, che ho fat-to i-o; os-ser-va-te, leg-ge-te con
gest it much fast-er If you skim through to-geth-er with

me! os-ser-va-te, leg-ge-te con me!
me: I main-tain it im-ma-cu-late-ly.

In I-ta-lia sei cen-to e qua-ran-ta;
Down for It-a-ly, six-hun-dred and for-ty;

No. 7: Duet: *Là ci darem la mano*

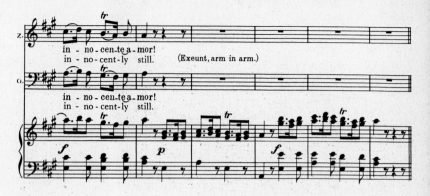

I

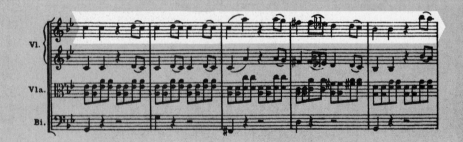

This edition presents the score of Mozart's second version, with clarinets.

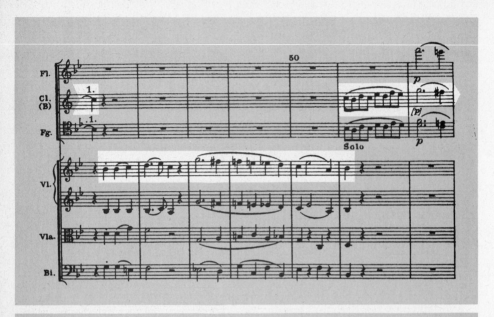

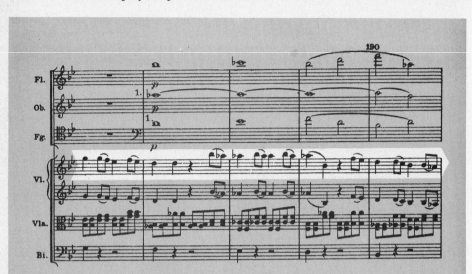

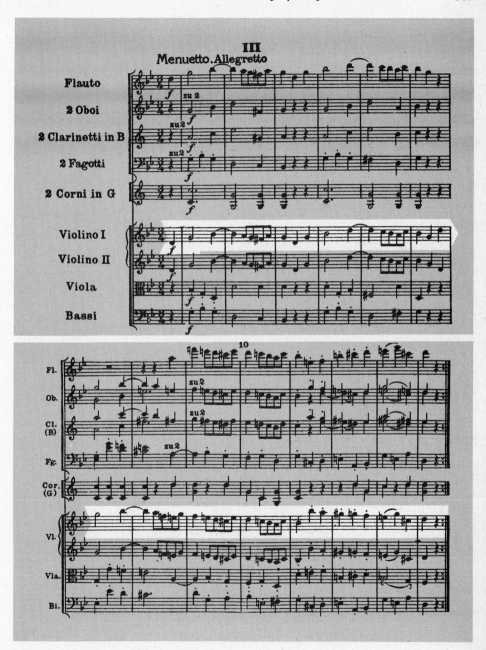

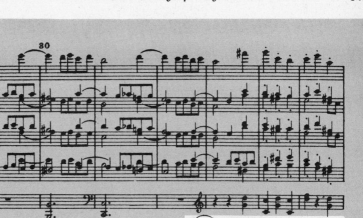

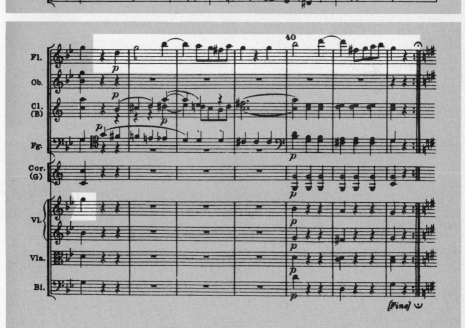

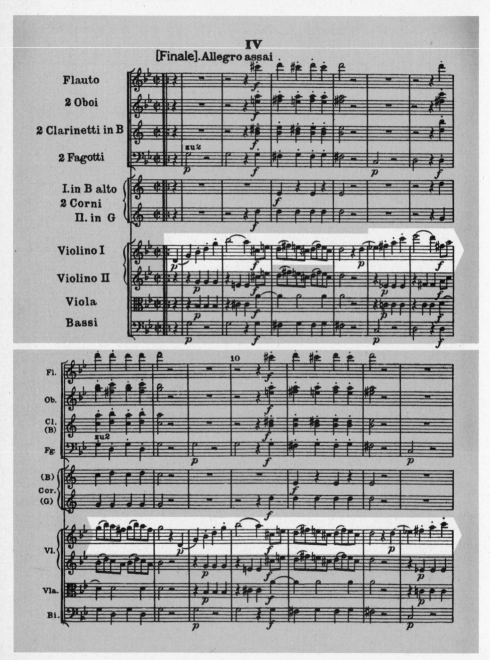

Fl.
Ob.
Cl. (B)
Fg.
zu 2
(B) Cor. (G)
Vl.
Vla.
Bi.

60
Fl.
Ob.
zu 2
Cl. (B)
zu 2
Fg.
zu 2
(B) Cor. (G)
Vl.
Vla.
Bi.

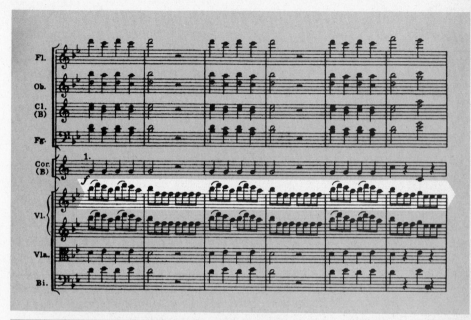

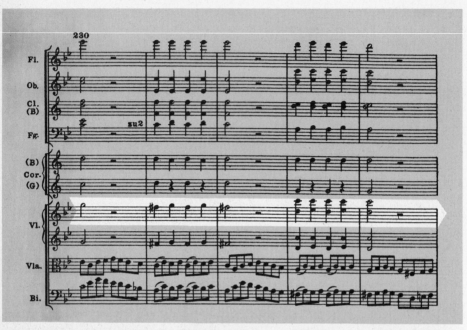

34. LUDWIG VAN BEETHOVEN (1770-1827),
First movement from *String Quartet in F major*, Opus 18, No. 1 (1798-1799)

16-2

35. BEETHOVEN,
Piano Sonata in C minor, Opus 13 (Pathétique) (1799)

attacca subito il Allegro.

36. BEETHOVEN, *Symphony No. 5 in C minor* (1807)

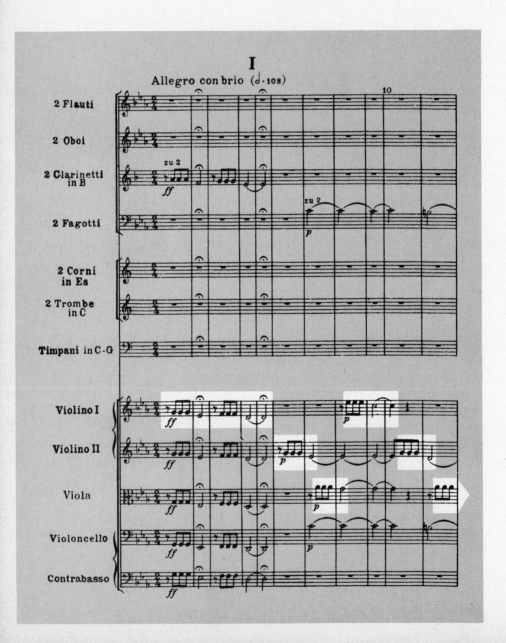

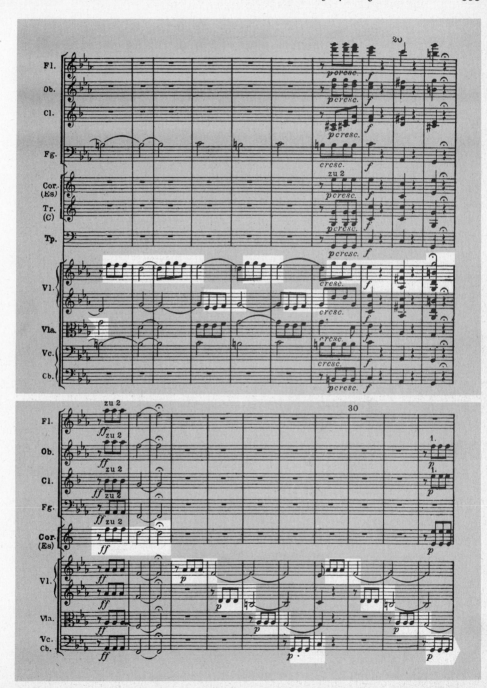

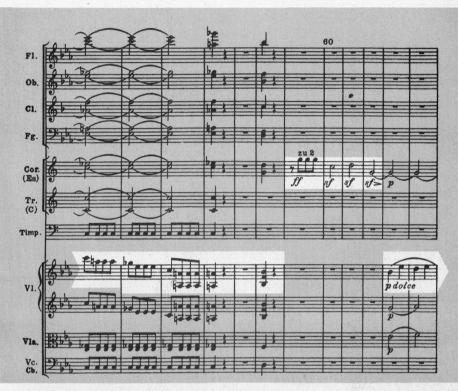

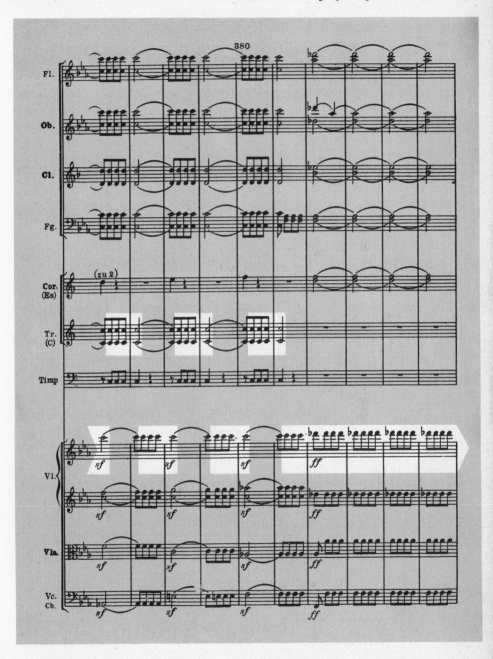

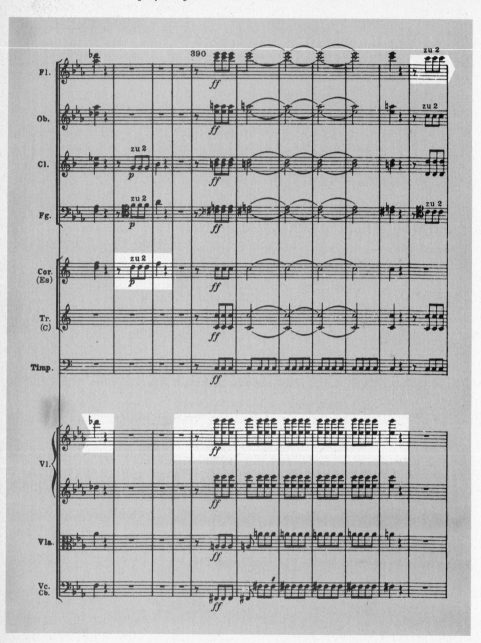

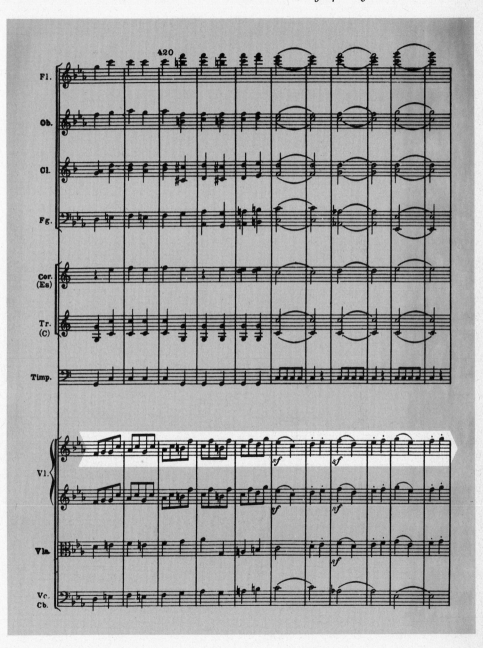

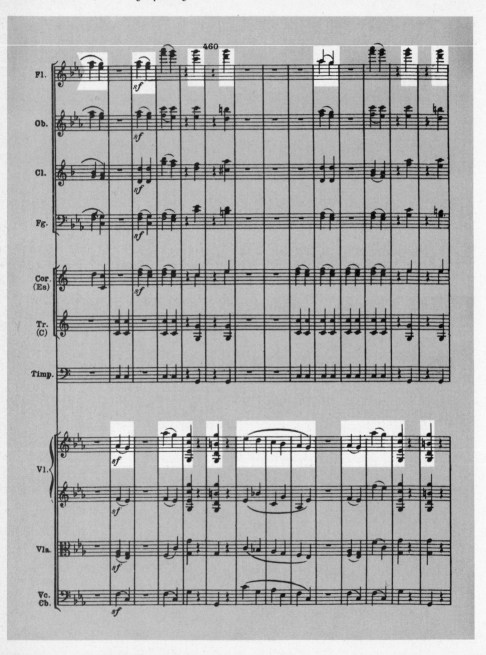

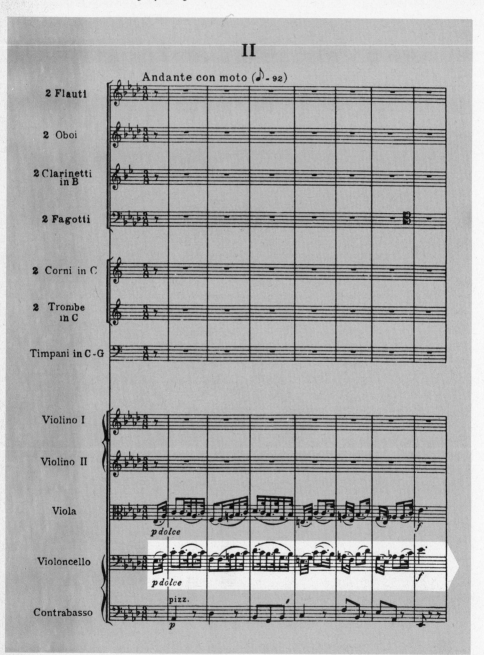

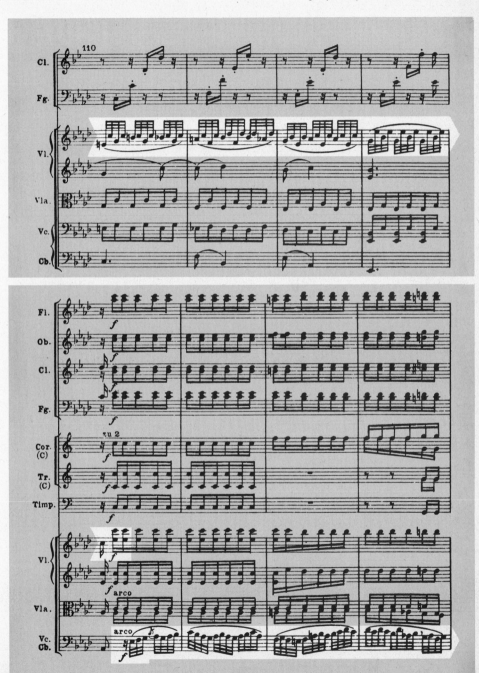

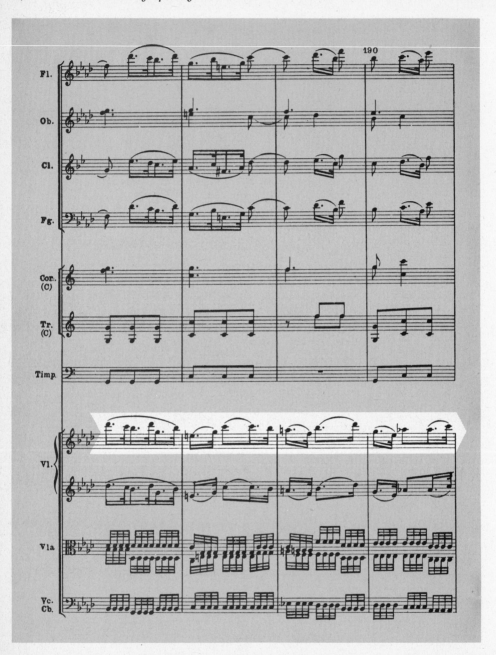

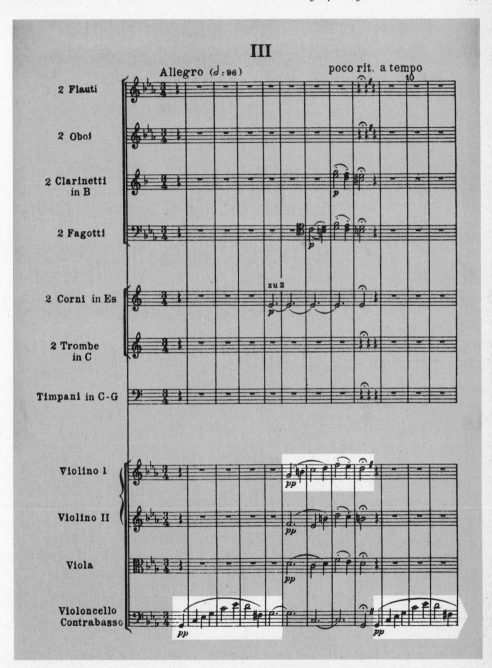

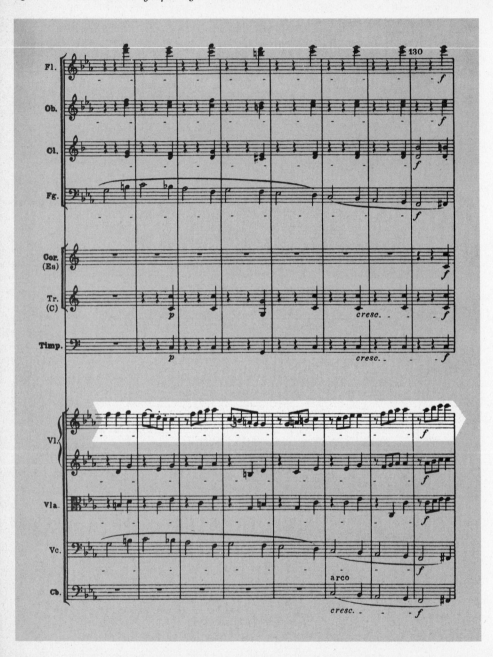

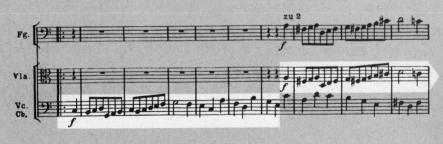

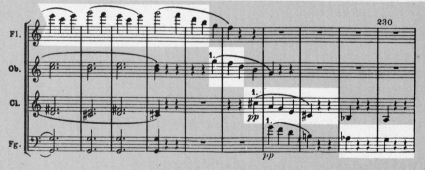

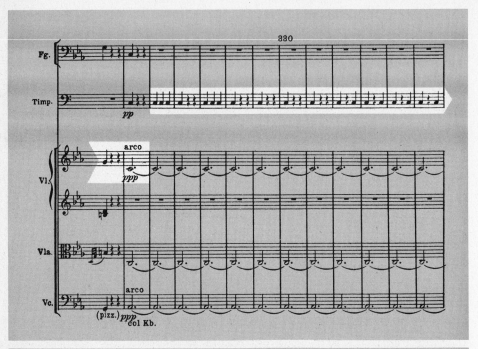

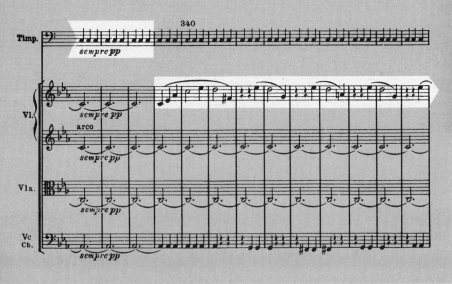

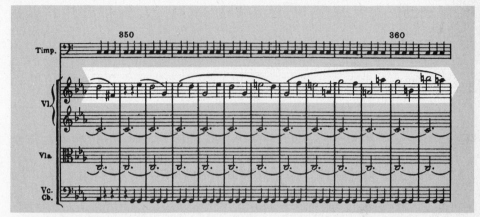

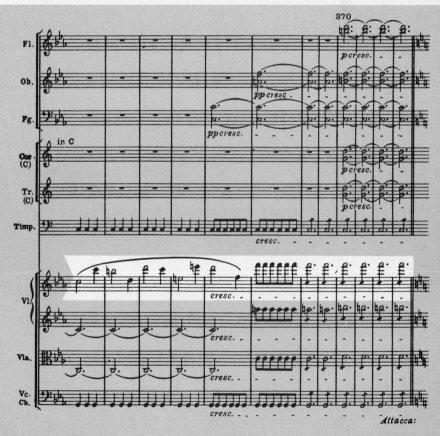

IV

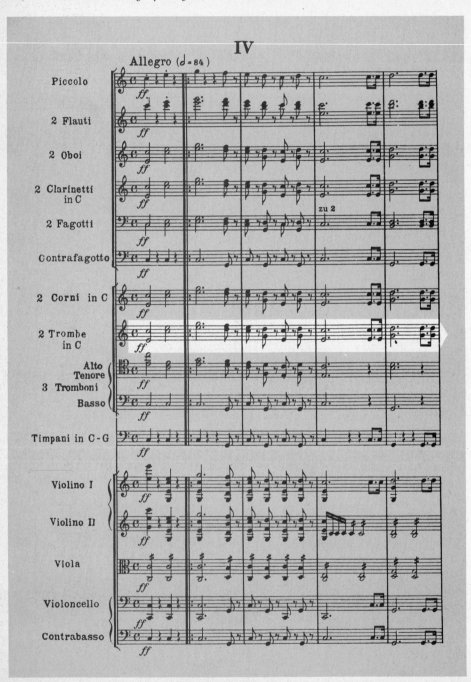

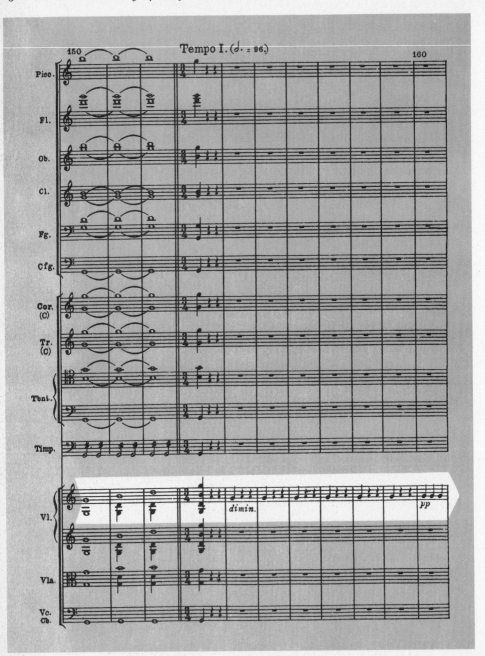

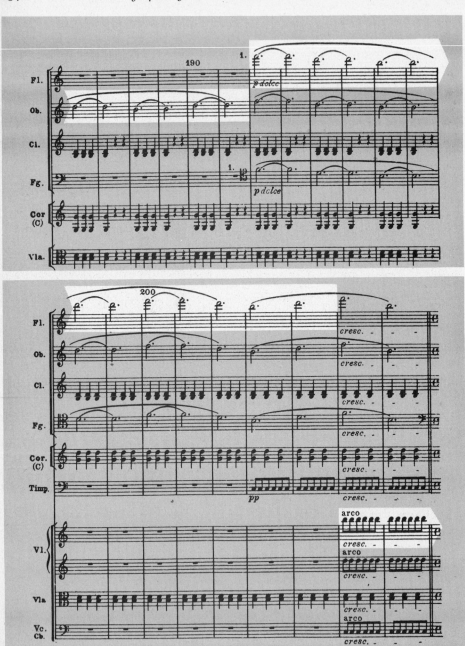

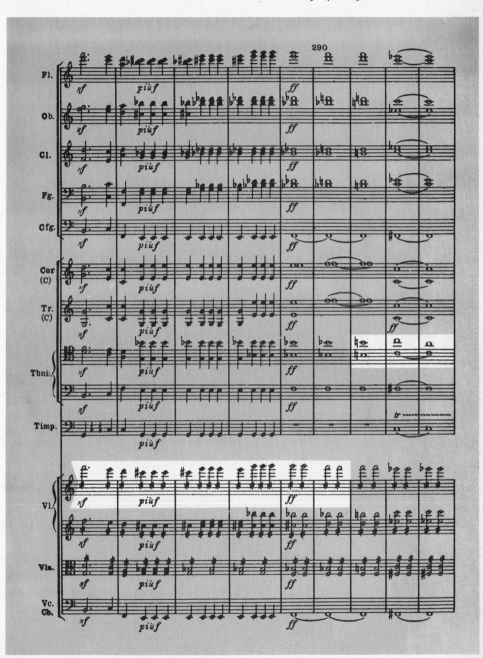

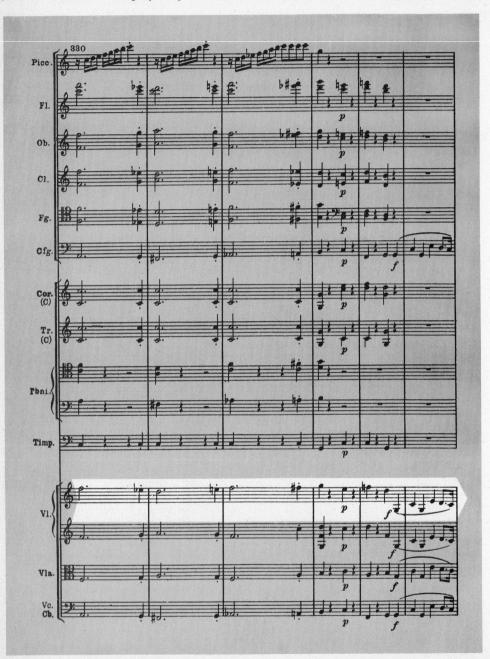

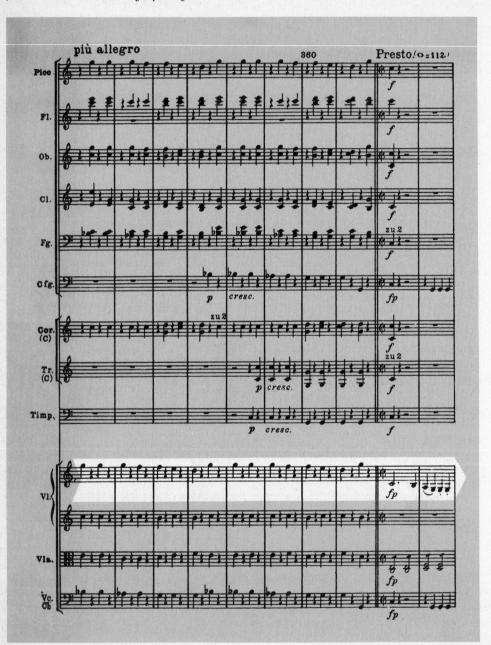

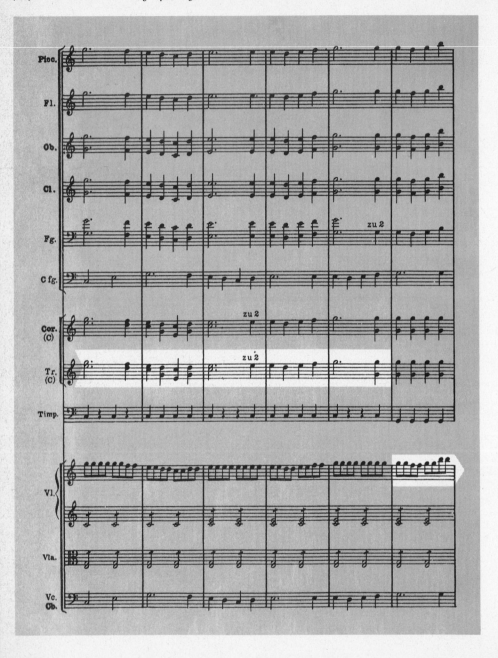

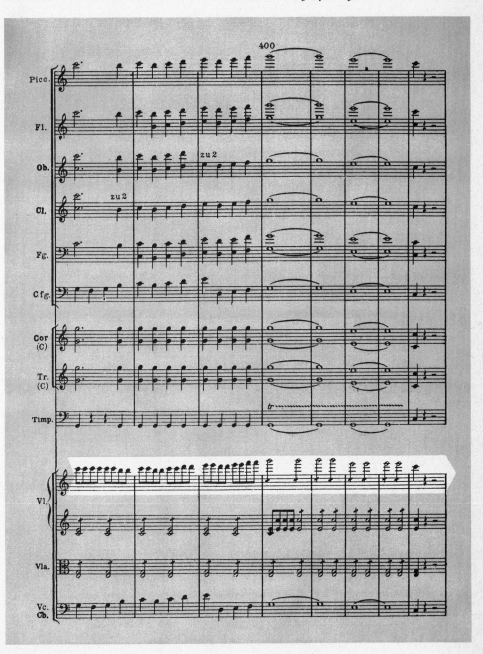

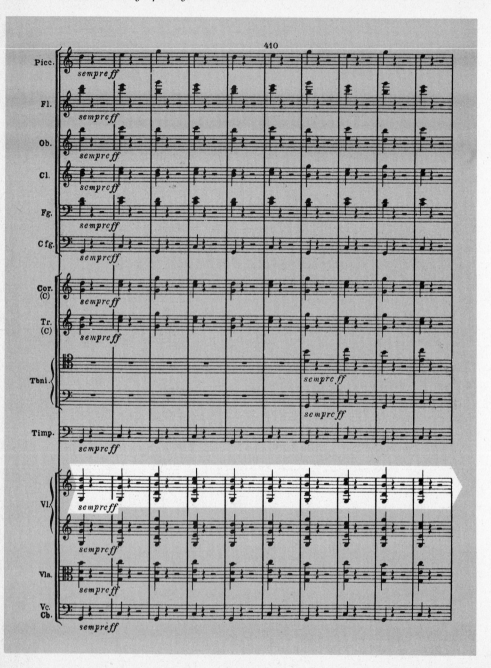

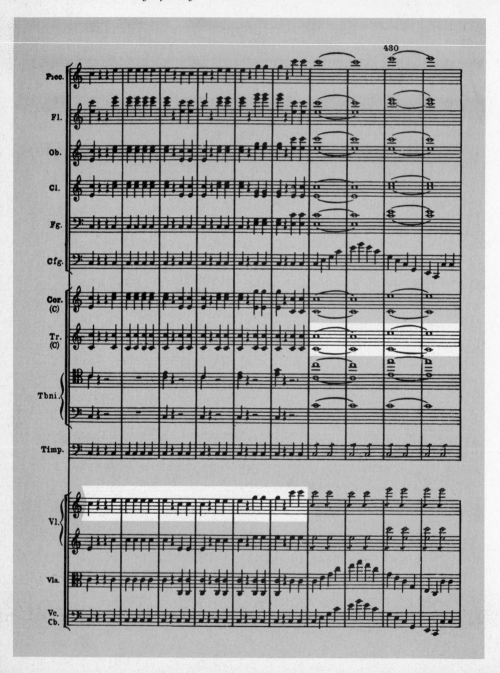

Appendix A

Reading an Orchestral Score

CLEFS

The music for some instruments is written in clefs other than the familiar treble and bass. In the following example, middle C is shown in the four clefs used in orchestral scores:

The *alto clef* is primarily used in viola parts. The *tenor clef* is employed for cello, bassoon, and trombone parts when these instruments play in a high register.

TRANSPOSING INSTRUMENTS

The music for some instruments is customarily written at a pitch different from their actual sound. The following list, with examples, shows the main transposing instruments and the degree of transposition. (In some modern works—such as the Schoenberg example included in this anthology —all instruments are written at their sounding pitch.)

Instrument	Transposition	Written Note	Actual Sound
Piccolo Celesta	sound an octave higher than written		
Trumpet in F	sound a fourth higher than written		
Trumpet in E	sound a major third higher than written		

Instrument	Transposition	Written Note	Actual Sound

Clarinet in Eb
  Trumpet in Eb
	sound a minor third
	  higher than written		

Trumpet in D
  Clarinet in D
	sound a major second
	  higher than written		

Clarinet in Bb
  Trumpet in Bb
  Cornet in Bb
  Horn in Bb alto
	sound a major second
	  lower than written		

Clarinet in A
  Trumpet in A
  Cornet in A
	sound a minor third
	  lower than written		

Horn in G
  Alto flute
	sound a fourth
	  lower than written		

English horn
  Horn in F
	sound a fifth
	  lower than written		

Horn in E	sound a minor sixth lower than written		
Horn in Eb	sound a major sixth lower than written		
Horn in D	sound a minor seventh lower than written		

Contrabassoon
  Horn in C
  Double bass
	sound an octave
	  lower than written		

Bass clarinet in Bb
  (written in treble clef)
	sound a major ninth
	  lower than written		

(written in bass clef)	sound a major second lower than written		

Bass clarinet in A
  (written in treble clef)
	sound a minor tenth
	  lower than written		

(written in bass clef)	sound a minor third lower than written		

Appendix B

Instrumental Names and Abbreviations

The following tables set forth the English, Italian, German, and French names used for the various musical instruments in these scores, and their respective abbreviations. A table of the foreign-language names for scale degrees and modes is also provided.

WOODWINDS

English	Italian	German	French
Piccolo (Picc.)	Flauto piccolo (Fl. Picc.)	Kleine Flöte (Kl. Fl.)	Petite flûte
Flute (Fl.)	Flauto (Fl.); Flauto grande (Fl. gr.)	Grosse Flöte (Fl. gr.)	Flûte (Fl.)
Alto flute	Flauto contralto (fl.c-alto)	Altflöte	Flûte en sol
Oboe (Ob.)	Oboe (Ob.)	Hoboe (Hb.); Oboe (Ob.)	Hautbois (Hb.)
English horn (E. H.)	Corno inglese (C. or Cor. ingl., C.i.)	Englisches Horn (E. H.)	Cor anglais (C. A.)
Sopranino clarinet	Clarinetto piccolo (clar. picc.)		
Clarinet (C., Cl., Clt., Clar.)	Clarinetto (Cl. Clar.)	Klarinette (Kl.)	Clarinette (Cl.)
Bass clarinet (B. Cl.)	Clarinetto basso (Cl. b., Cl. basso, Clar. basso)	Bass Klarinette (Bkl.)	Clarinette basse (Cl. bs.)
Bassoon (Bsn., Bssn.)	Fagotto (Fag., Fg.)	Fagott (Fag., Fg.)	Basson (Bssn.)
Contrabassoon (C. Bsn.)	Contrafagotto (Cfg., C. Fag., Cont. F.)	Kontrafagott (Kfg.)	Contrebasson (C. bssn.)

BRASS

English	Italian	German	French
French horn (Hr., Hn.)	Corno (Cor., C.)	Horn (Hr.) [*pl.* Hörner (Hrn.)]	Cor; Cor à pistons
Trumpet (Tpt., Trpt., Trp., Tr.)	Tromba (Tr.)	Trompete (Tr., Trp.)	Trompette (Tr.)
Trumpet in D	Tromba piccola (Tr. picc.)		
Cornet	Cornetta	Kornett	Cornet à pistons (C. à p., Pist.)
Trombone (Tr., Tbe., Trb., Trm., Trbe.)	Trombone [*pl.* Tromboni (Tbni., Trni.)]	Posaune (Ps., Pos.)	Trombone (Tr.)
Tuba (Tb.)	Tuba (Tb, Tba:)	Tuba (Tb.) [*also* Basstuba (Btb.)]	Tuba (Tb.)

PERCUSSION

English	Italian	German	French
Percussion (Perc.)	Percussione	Schlagzeug (Schlag.)	Batterie (Batt.)
Kettledrums (K. D.)	Timpani (Timp., Tp.)	Pauken (Pk.)	Timbales (Timb.)
Snare drum (S. D.)	Tamburo piccolo (Tamb. picc.) Tamburo militare (Tamb. milit.)	Kleine Trommel (Kl. Tr.)	Caisse claire (C. cl.), Caisse roulante Tambour militaire (Tamb. milit.)
Bass drum (B. drum)	Gran cassa (Gr. Cassa, Gr. C., G. C.)	Grosse Trommel (Gr. Tr.)	Grosse caisse (Gr. c.)
Cymbals (Cym., Cymb.)	Piatti (P., Ptti., Piat.)	Becken (Beck.)	Cymbales (Cym.)
Tam-Tam (Tam-T.)			
Tambourine (Tamb.)	Tamburino (Tamb.)	Schellentrommel, Tamburin	Tambour de Basque (T. de B., Tamb. de Basque)

Triangle (Trgl., Tri.)	Triangolo (Trgl.)	Triangel	Triangle (Triang.)
Glockenspiel (Glocken.)	Campanelli (Cmp.)	Glockenspiel	Carillon
Bells (Chimes)	Campane (Cmp.)	Glocken	Cloches
Antique Cymbals	Crotali Piatti antichi	Antiken Zimbeln	Cymbales antiques
Sleigh Bells	Sonagli (Son.)	Schellen	Grelots
Xylophone (Xyl.)	Xilofono	Xylophon	Xylophone
Cowbells		Herdenglocken	
Crash cymbal			Grande cymbale chinoise
Siren			Sirène
Lion's roar			Tambour à corde
Slapstick			Fouet
Wood blocks			Blocs chinois

STRINGS

English	*Italian*	*German*	*French*
Violin (V., Vl., Vln, Vi.)	Violino (V., Vl., Vln.)	Violine (V., Vl., Vln.) Geige (Gg.)	Violon (V., Vl., Vln.)
Viola (Va., Vl., *pl.* Vas.)	Viola (Va., Vla.) *pl.* Viole (Vle.)	Bratsche (Br.)	Alto (A.)
Violoncello, Cello (Vcl., Vc.)	Violoncello (Vc., Vlc., Vcllo.)	Violoncell (Vc., Vlc.)	Violoncelle (Vc.)
Double bass (D. Bs.)	Contrabasso (Cb., C. B.) *pl.* Contrabassi or Bassi (C. Bassi, Bi.)	Kontrabass (Kb.)	Contrebasse (C. B.)

OTHER INSTRUMENTS

English	*Italian*	*German*	*French*
Harp (Hp., Hrp.)	Arpa (A., Arp.)	Harfe (Hrf.)	Harpe (Hp.)
Piano	Pianoforte (P.-f., Pft.)	Klavier	Piano
Celesta (Cel.)			
Harpsichord	Cembalo	Cembalo	Clavecin
Harmonium (Harmon.)			
Organ (Org.)	Organo	Orgel	Orgue
Guitar		Gitarre (Git.)	
Mandoline (Mand.)			

Names of Scale Degrees and Modes

SCALE DEGREES

English	Italian	German	French
C	do	C	ut
C-sharp	do diesis	Cis	ut dièse
D-flat	re bemolle	Des	ré bémol
D	re	D	ré
D-sharp	re diesis	Dis	ré dièse
E-flat	mi bemolle	Es	mi bémol
E	mi	E	mi
E-sharp	mi diesis	Eis	mi dièse
F-flat	fa bemolle	Fes	fa bémol
F	fa	F	fa
F-sharp	fa diesis	Fis	fa dièse
G-flat	sol bemolle	Ges	sol bémol
G	sol	G	sol
G-sharp	sol diesis	Gis	sol dièse
A-flat	la bemolle	As	la bémol
A	la	A	la
A-sharp	la diesis	Ais	la dièse
B-flat	si bemolle	B	si bémol
B	si	H	si
B-sharp	si diesis	His	si dièse
C-flat	do bemolle	Ces	ut bémol

MODES

major	maggiore	dur	majeur
minor	minore	moll	mineur

Note on Baroque Instruments

In the Baroque works, certain older instruments, not used in the modern orchestra, were required by the composers; the following list defines these terms.

Continuo (Con.) A method of indicating an accompanying part by the bass notes only, together with figures designating the chords to be played above them. In general practice, the chords are played on a harpsichord or organ, while a viola da gamba or cello doubles the bass notes.

and a bass lute (as continuo instruments).

Corno. Although this term usually designates the French horn, in the Bach Cantata No. 140 it refers to the *cornett,* or *zink*—a wooden trumpet without valves.

Taille (Tail.). In the Bach Cantata No. 140, this term indicates a tenor oboe or English horn.

Violino piccolo. A small violin, tuned a fourth higher than the standard violin.

Violone (V.). A string instrument intermediate in size between the cello and the double bass. (In modern performances, the double bass is commonly substituted.)

Appendix C

Glossary of Musical Terms Used in the Scores

The following glossary is not intended to be a complete dictionary of musical terms, nor is knowledge of all these terms necessary to follow the scores in this book. However, as the listener gains experience in following scores, he will find it useful and interesting to understand the composer's directions with regard to tempo, dynamics, and methods of performance.

In most cases, compound terms have been broken down in the glossary and defined separately, as they often recur in varying combinations. A few common foreign-language particles are included in addition to the musical terms. Note that names and abbreviations for instruments and for scale degrees will be found in Appendix B.

a. The phrases *a 2, a 3* (etc.) indicate that the part is to be played in unison by 2, 3 (etc.) players; when a simple number (1., 2., etc.) is placed over a part, it indicates that only the first (second, etc.) player in that group should play.

aber. But.

accelerando. Growing faster.

accentué. Accented.

accompagnato (accomp.). In a continuo part, this indicates that the chord-playing instrument resumes (cf. *tasto solo*).

accordez. Tune the instrument as specified.

adagio. Slow, leisurely.

ad libitum (ad lib.). An indication giving the performer liberty to: (1) vary from strict tempo; (2) include or omit the part of some voice or instrument; (3) include a cadenza of his own invention.

affettuoso. With emotion.

affrettando (affrett.). Hastening a little.

agitato. Agitated, excited.

agitazione. Agitation.

allargando (allarg.). Growing broader.

alle, alles. All, every, each.

allegretto. A moderately fast tempo (between allegro and andante).

allegro. A rapid tempo (between allegretto and presto).

allein. Alone, solo.

allmählich. Gradually (*allmählich gleichmässig fliessend werden,* gradually becoming even-flowing again).

al niente. Reduce to nothing.

alto, altus (A.). The deeper of the two main divisions of women's (or boys') voices.

am Steg. On the bridge (of a string instrument).

ancora. Again.

andante. A moderately slow tempo (between adagio and allegretto).

andantino. A moderately slow tempo.

an dem Griffbrett (a.d.G.). Played on the fingerboard.

anima. Spirit, animation.

animando. With increasing animation.

animato, animé. Animated.

a piacere. The execution of the passage is left to the performer's discretion.

à plat. Laid flat.

appassionato. Impassioned.

arco. Played with the bow.

arditamente. Boldly.

armonioso. Harmoniously.

arpeggiando, arpeggiato (arpeg.). Played in harp style, i.e. the notes of the chord played in quick succession rather than simultaneously.

arrêt. Stop.

assai. Very.

a tempo. At the (basic) tempo.

attacca. Begin what follows without pausing.

attaque sèche. Sharp attack.

auf dem. On the (as in *auf dem G,* on the G string).

Ausdruck. Expression.

ausdrucksvoll. With expression.

bachetti. Drumsticks (*bachetti di tamburo militare,* snare-drum sticks; *bachetti di spugna,* sponge-headed drumsticks).

baguettes. Drumsticks (*baguettes de bois, baguettes timbales de bois,* wooden drumsticks or kettledrum sticks; *baguettes d'éponge,* sponge-headed drumsticks; *baguettes midures,* semi-hard drumsticks; *baguettes dures,* hard drumsticks; *baguettes timbales en feutre,* felt-headed kettledrum sticks).

bass, basso, bassus (B.). The lowest male voice.

battuto coll' arco. Struck with the bow.

beaucoup. Many, much.

bedeutung bewegter. With significantly more movement.

beide Hände. With both hands.

belebend. With increasing animation.

belebt. Animated.

ben. Very.

ben accordato. Well tuned.

bestimmt. Energetic.

bewegt. Agitated.

bewegter. More agitated.

bien. Very.

bis zum Schluss dieser Szene. To the end of this scene.

Blech. Brass instruments.

Bogen (Bog.). Played with the bow.

bouché. Muted.

bravura. Boldness.

breit. Broadly.

breiter. More broadly.

brillante. Brilliant.

brio. Spirit, vivacity.

cadenza. An extended passage for solo instrument in free, improvisatory style.

calando. Diminishing in volume and speed.

calma, calmo. Calm, calmly.

cantabile (cant.). In a singing style.

cantando. In a singing manner.

canto. Voice (as in *col canto,* a direction for the accompaniment to follow the solo part in tempo and expression).

cantus. An older designation for the highest part in a vocal work.

capella. Choir, chorus.

cédez. Go a little slower.

changez. Change (usually an instruction to re-tune a string or an instrument).

circa (ca.). About, approximately.

clair. High.

col, colla, coll'. With the.

come prima, come sopra. As at first; as previously.

con. With.

corda. String; for example, *seconda (2a) corda* is the second string (the A string on the violin).

coro. Chorus.

coulisse. Wings (of a theater).

court. Short, staccato.

crescendo (cresc.). An increase in volume.

cuivré. Played with a harsh, blaring tone.

cum quatuor vocibus. With four voices.

cupo. Dark, veiled.

da capo (D.C.). Repeat from the beginning.

dal segno. Repeat from the sign.

Dämpfer (Dpf.). Mutes.

dans. In.

dazu. In addition to that, for that purpose.

début. Beginning.

decrescendo (decresc., decr.). A decreasing of volume.

descendez le "la" un demi-ton plus bas. Lower the A-string a semitone.

détaché. With a broad, vigorous bow stroke, each note bowed singly.

détimbrée. With snares (of a snare drum) relaxed.

deutlich. Distinctly.

dimenuendo, diminuer (dim., dimin.). A decreasing of volume.

distinto. Distinct, clear.

divisés, divisi (div.). Divided; indicates that the instrumental group should be divided into two parts to play the passage in question.

dolce. Sweetly and softly.

dolcemente. Sweetly.

dolcissimo (dolciss.). Very sweetly.

Doppelgriff. Double stop.

doppio movimento. Twice as fast.

doux. Sweetly.

drängend. Pressing on.

duplum. In older music, the part immediately above the tenor.

durée indiquée. The duration indicated.

e. And.

eilen. To hurry.

en animant. Becoming more animated.

enchainez. Continue to the next material without pause.

en dehors. With emphasis.

energico. Energetically.

ersterbend. Dying away.

erstes Tempo. At the original tempo.

espansione. Expansion, broadening.

espressione intensa. Intense expression.

espressivo (espress., espr.). Expressively.

et. And.

etwas. Somewhat, rather.

expressif. Expressively.

fehlende Akkordtöne. Missing chord tones.

fiero. Fiercely.

fine. End, close.

Flageolett (Flag.). Harmonics.

flatterzunge, flutter-tongue. A special tonguing technique for wind instruments, producing a rapid trill-like sound.

fliessend. Flowing.

forte (f). Loud.

fortissimo (ff). Very loud (*fff* indicates a still louder dynamic).

forza. Force.

frei. Freely.

freihäng. Hanging freely. An indication to the percussionist to let the cymbals vibrate feely.

frottez. Rub.

fuga. Fugue.

fuoco. Fire, spirit.

furioso. Furiously.

gajo. Gaily.

ganz. Entirely, altogether.

ganzton. Whole tone.

gedämpft (ged.). Muted.

geheimnisvoll. Mysteriously.

gesteigert. Intensified.

gestopft (chiuso). Stopping the notes of a horn; that is, the hand is placed in the bell of the horn, to produce a muffled sound.

geteilt (get.). Divided; indicates that the instrumental group should be divided into two parts to play the passage in question.

giocoso. Jocose, humorous.

giusto. Moderately.

gli altri. The others.

glissando (gliss.). Rapid scales produced by running the fingers over all the strings.

gradamente. Gradually.

grande. Large, great.

grande taille. Large size.

grave. Slow, solemn; deep, low.

grazioso. Gracefully.

grosser Auftakt. Big upbeat.

gut gehalten. Well sustained.

H. A symbol used in the music of Schoenberg, Berg, and Webern to indicate the most important voice in the texture.

Hälfte. Half.

harmonic (harm.). A flute-like sound produced on a string instrument by lightly touching the string with the finger instead of pressing it down.

Hauptzeitmass. Original tempo.

heimlich. Furtively.

hervortretend. Prominent.

hoch. High; nobly.

Holz. Woodwinds.

im gleichen Rhythmus. In the same rhythm.

immer chromatisch. Always chromatic.

immer im Tempo. Always in tempo.

in neuen Tempo. In the new tempo.

istesso tempo. Duration of beat remains unaltered despite meter change.

jeté. With a bouncing motion of the bow.

jusqu'à la fin. To the end.

kadenzieren. To cadence.

kaum hörbar. Barely audible.

klagend. Lamenting.

kurz. Short.

laissez vibrer. Let vibrate; an indication to the player of a harp, cymbal, etc., that the sound must not be damped.

langsam. Slow.

langsamer. Slower.

languente. Languishing.

langueur. Languor.

largamente. Broadly.

larghetto. Slightly faster than largo.

largo. A very slow tempo.

lebhaft. Lively.

leere Bühne. Empty stage.

legatissimo. A more forceful indication of *legato.*

legato. Performed without any perceptible interruption between notes.

légèrement. Lightly.

leggèro, leggiero (legg.). Light and graceful.

legno. The wood of the bow (*col legno tratto,* bowed with the wood; *col legno battuto,* tapped with the wood; *col legno gestrich,* played with the wood).

leise. Soft, low.

lent. Slowly.

lentamente. Slowly.

lento. A slow tempo (between andante and largo).

l.h. Abbreviation for "left hand."

lieblich. Lovely, sweetly.

loco. Indicates a return to the written pitch, following a passage played an octave higher or lower than written.

lontano. Far away, from a distance.

luftpause. Pause for breath.

lunga. Long, sustained.

lungo silenzio. A long pause.

ma. But.

maestoso. Majestic.

manual. A keyboard played with the hands (as distinct from the pedal keyboard on an organ).

marcatissimo (marcatiss.). With very marked emphasis.

marcato (marc.). Marked, with emphasis.

marcia. March.

marqué. Marked, with emphasis.

mässig. Moderate.

même. Same.

meno. Less.

mezza voce. With half the voice power.

mezzo forte (mf). Moderately loud.

mezzo piano (mp). Moderately soft.

mindistens. At least.

minore. In the minor mode.

mit. With.

M. M. Metronome; followed by an indication of the setting for the correct tempo.

moderato, modéré. At a moderate tempo.

modo ordinario (ordin.). In the usual way (usually cancelling an instruction to play using some special technique).

molto. Very, much.

morendo. Dying away.

mormorato. Murmured.

mosso. Rapid.

motetus. In medieval polyphonic music, a voice part above the tenor; generally, the first additional part to be composed.

moto. Motion.

mouvement (mouvt.). Tempo.

moyenne. Medium.

muta, mutano. Change the tuning of the instrument as specified.

N. A symbol used in the music of Schoenberg, Berg, and Webern to indicate the second most important voice in the texture.

nachgebend. Becoming slower.

nach und nach. More and more.

naturalezza. A natural, unaffected manner.

naturel. In the usual way (generally cancelling an instruction to play using some special technique).

nicht, non. Not.

noch. Still.

nuances. Shadings, expression.

oberer. Upper, leading.

octava (8va). Octave; if not otherwise qualified, means the notes marked should be played an octave higher than written.

octava bassa (8va bassa). Play an octave lower than written.

ohne. Without.

open. (1) In brass instruments, the opposite of muted; (2) in string instruments, refers to the unstopped string (i.e. sounding at its full length).

ordinario, ordinérement (ordin.). In the usual way (generally cancelling an instruction to play using some special technique).

ossia. An alternative (usually easier) version of a passage.

ôtez vite les sourdines. Remove the mutes quickly.

ouvert. Open.

parlante. Sung in a manner resembling speech.

parte. Part (*colla parte,* the accompaniment is to follow the soloist in tempo).

pas trop long. Not too long.

Paukenschlägel. Timpani stick.

pavillon en l'aire. An indication to the player of a wind instrument to raise the bell of the instrument upward.

pedal (ped., P.). (1) In piano music, indicates that the damper pedal should be depressed; an asterisk indicates the point of release (brackets below the music are also used to indicate pedalling); (2) on an organ, the pedals are a keyboard played with the feet.

percutée. Percussive.

perdendosi. Gradually dying away.

pesante. Heavily.

peu. Little, a little.

pianissimo (pp). Very soft (*ppp* indicates a still softer dynamic).

piano (p). Soft.

più. More.

pizzicato (pizz.). The string plucked with the finger.

plötzlich. Suddenly, immediately.

plus. More.

pochissimo (pochiss.). Very little, a very little.

poco. Little, a little.

poco a poco. Little by little.

ponticello (pont.). The bridge (of a string instrument).

portando la voce. With a smooth sliding of the voice from one tone to the next.

position naturel (pos. nat.). In the normal position (usually cancelling an instruction to play using some special technique).

pouce. Thumb.

pour. For.

praeludium. Prelude.

premier mouvement (1er mouvt.). At the original tempo.

prenez. Take up.

préparez le ton. Prepare the instrument to play in the key named.

presser. To press.

presto. A very quick tempo (faster than allegro).

principale (pr.). Principal, solo.

punta d'arco. Played with the top of the bow.

quasi. Almost, as if.

quasi niente. Almost nothing, i.e. as softly as possible.

quasi trill (tr.). In the manner of a trill.

quintus. An older designation for the fifth part in a vocal work.

rallentando (rall., rallent.). Growing slower.

rapide, rapido. Quick.

rapidissimo. Very quick.

rasch. Quick.

rauschend. Rustling, roaring.

recitative (recit.). A vocal style designed to imitate and emphasize the natural inflections of speech.

retenu. Held back.

revenir au Tempo. Return to the original tempo.

richtig. Correct (*richtige Lage,* correct pitch).

rigore di tempo. Strictness of tempo.

rigueur. Precision.

risoluto. Determined.

ritardando (rit., ritard.). Gradually slackening in speed.

ritenuto (riten.). Immediate reduction of speed.

rubato. A certain elasticity and flexibility of tempo, consisting of slight accelerandos and ritardandos according to the requirements of the musical expression.

ruhig. Quietly.

rullante. Rolling.

saltando (salt.). An indication to the string player to bounce the bow off the string by playing with short, quick bow-strokes.

sans timbre. Without snares.

scena vuota. Empty stage.

scherzando (scherz.). Playful.

schleppend. Dragging.

Schluss. Cadence, conclusion.

schmachtend. Languishing.

schnell. Fast.

schneller. Faster.

schon. Already.

scorrevole. Flowing, gliding.

sec, secco. Dry, simple.

seconda volta. The second time.

segue. (1) Continue to the next movement without pausing; (2) continue in the same manner.

sehr. Very.

semplicità. Simplicity.

sempre. Always, continually.

senza. Without.

sforzando, sforzato (sfz, sf). With sudden emphasis.

sfumato. Diminishing and fading away.

simile. In a similar manner.

Singstimme. Singing voice.

sino al. Up to the . . . (usually followed by a new tempo marking, or by a dotted line indicating a terminal point).

smorzando (smorz.). Dying away.

sofort. Immediately.

solo (s.). Executed by one performer.

sonator. Player (*uno sonator,* one player; *due sonatori,* two players).

sonné à la double 8va. Play the double octave.

sopra. Above; in piano music, used to indicate that one hand must pass above the other.

soprano (S.). The voice classification with the highest range.

sordino (sord.). Mute.

sostenendo, sostenuto. Sustained.

sotto voce. In an undertone, subdued, under the breath.

sourdine. Mute.

soutenu. Sustained.

spiccato. With a light bouncing motion of the bow.

spiritoso. In a spirited manner.

staccatissimo. Very staccato.

staccato (stacc.). Detached, separated, abruptly disconnected.

stentando, stentato (stent.). Delaying, retarding.

stesso movimento. The same basic pace.

stretto. In a non-fugal composition, indicates a concluding section at an increased speed.

stringendo (string.). Quickening.

subito (sub.). Suddenly, immediately.

sul. On the (as in *sul G,* on the G string).

suono. Sound, tone.

superius. In older music, the uppermost part.

sur. On.

suspendue. Suspended.

tacet. The instrument or vocal part so marked is silent.

tasto solo. In a continuo part, this indicates that only the string instrument plays; the chord-playing instrument is silent.

tempo primo (tempo I). At the original tempo.

tenor, tenore (T.). The highest male voice.

tenuto (ten.). Held, sustained.

tief. Deep, low.

tornando al tempo primo. Returning to the original tempo.

touch. Fingerboard (of a string instrument).

toujours. Always, continually.

tranquillo. Quietly, calmly.

tre corda (t.c.). Release the soft (or *una corda*) pedal of the piano.

tremolo (trem). On string instruments, a quick reiteration of the same tone, produced by a rapid up-and-down movement of the bow; also a rapid alternation between two different notes.

très. Very.

trill (tr.). The rapid alternation of a given note with the diatonic second above it. In a drum part it indicates rapid alternating strokes with two drumsticks.

triplum. In medieval polyphonic music, a voice part above the tenor.

troppo. Too much.

tutta la forza. Very emphatically.

tutti. Literally, "all"; usually means all the instruments in a given category as distinct from a solo part.

übergreifen. To overlap.

übertönend. Drowning out.

una corda (u.c.). With the "soft" pedal of the piano depressed.

und. And.

unison (unis.). The same notes or melody played by several instruments at the same pitch. Often used to emphasize that a phrase is not to be divided among several players.

verhallend. Fading away.

verklingen lassen. To let die away.

verlöschend. Extinguishing.

vierhändig. Four-hand piano music.

vif. Lively.

vivace. Quick, lively.

vivo. Lively.

voce. Voice (as in *colla voce,* a direction for the accompaniment to follow the solo part in tempo and expression).

voilà. There.

Vorhang auf. Curtain up.

Vorhang fällt, Vorhang zu. Curtain down.

voriges. Preceding.

Walzertempo. In the tempo of a waltz.

weg. Away, beyond.

weich. Mellow, smooth, soft.

weiter. Further, forward.

wie aus der Ferne. As if from afar.

wieder. Again.

wie oben. As above, as before.

wie zu Anfang dieser Szene. As at the beginning of this scene.

wüthend. Furiously.

zart. Tenderly, delicately.

Zeitmass. Tempo.

zögernd. Slower.

zu. The phrases *zu 2, zu 3* (etc.) indicate that the part is to be played in unison by 2, 3 (etc.) players.

zurückhaltend. Slackening in speed.

zurücktreten. To withdraw.

zweihändig. With two hands.

Index of Forms and Genres

A roman numeral following a title indicates a movement within the work named.

A-B-A form: *see* ternary form
A-B form: *see* binary form
a capella music:
GREGORIAN CHANTS, *Gaudeamus omnes* (p. 3); *Kyrie XII* (p. 5); *Kyrie IV* (p. 7); *Alma redemptoris mater* (p. 12); *Requiem aeternam* (p. 22)
ANONYMOUS, *O miranda dei karitas —Salva mater salutifera—Kyrie* (p. 5)
MACHAUT, *Messe de Notre Dame* (p. 7)
DUFAY, *Alma redemptoris mater* (p. 12)
BUSNOIS, *Amour nous traicte—Je me'n vois* (p. 18)
JOSQUIN, *Déploration sur la mort de Johan Okeghem* (p. 22); *Scaramella* (p. 30); *Missa L'homme armé* (p. 32)
ANONYMOUS, *L'homme armé* (p. 32)
ARCADELT, *Il bianco cigno* (p. 46)
PALESTRINA, *Missa Ascendo ad Patrem* (p. 49)
LASSUS, *Prophetiae sibyllarum* p. 55)
MORLEY, *Sing We and Chant It* (p. 60)
GABRIELI, *Nunc dimittis* (p. 62)
WEELKES, *As Vesta Was Descending* (p. 89)

Agnus Dei:
JOSQUIN, *Missa L'homme armé,* Agnus Dei (p. 32)
allemande:
CORELLI, *Trio Sonata,* Op. 4, No. 1/III (p. 116)
aria:
PURCELL, *Dido and Aeneas,* Dido's Lament (p. 118)
HANDEL, *Giulio Cesare,* Piangerò (p. 147); *Messiah,* Ev'ry valley (p. 157)
GLUCK, *Orfeo ed Euridice,* Che farò senza Euridice? (p. 291)
MOZART, *Don Giovanni,* Introduction (p. 475), Catalogue Aria (p. 487)
arioso:
HANDEL, *Messiah,* Comfort ye (p. 154)

binary form:
CORELLI, *Trio Sonata,* Op. 4, No. 1/II, III (pp. 114, 116)
BACH, *Suite No. 3,* Air and Gigue (p. 226); *Cantata No. 140/VII* (p. 284)
SCARLATTI, *Sonata in C minor* (p. 289)

cadenza (point of insertion):
MOZART, *Piano Concerto in D* (pp. 405, 447)

cantata:
BACH, *Cantata No. 140* (p. 234)
chaconne: *see* ground bass
chamber music:
CORELLI, *Trio Sonata*, Op. 4, No. 1 (p. 113)
MOZART, *Eine kleine Nachtmusik* (p. 451)
BEETHOVEN, *String Quartet*, Op. 18, No. 1 (p. 566)
chanson:
BUSNOIS, *Amour nous traicte—Je m'en vois* (p. 18)
chant:
Gaudeamus omnes (p. 3); *Kyrie XII* (p. 5); *Kyrie IV* (p. 7); *Alma redemptoris mater* (p. 12); *Requiem aeternam* (p. 22)
choral music:
MACHAUT, *Messe de Notre Dame* (p. 7)
DUFAY, *Alma redemptoris mater* (p. 12)
JOSQUIN, *Déploration sur la mort de Johan Okeghem* (p. 22); *Missa L'homme armé* (p. 32)
PALESTRINA, *Missa Ascendo ad Patrem* (p. 49)
LASSUS, *Prophetiae sibyllarum* (p. 55)
MORLEY, *Sing We and Chant It* (p. 60)
GABRIELI, *Nunc dimittis* (p. 62)
MONTEVERDI, *L'Orfeo, Ahi, caso acerbo* (p. 76)
WEELKES, *As Vesta Was Descending* (p. 89)
SCHÜTZ, *Saul* (p. 99)
HANDEL, *Messiah, For unto us a Child is born* (p. 163); *Hallelujah* (p. 174)
BACH, *Cantata No. 140/I, IV, VII* (pp. 234, 272, 284)

chorale:
BACH, *Cantata No. 140/I, IV, VII* (pp. 234, 272, 284)
chorus, operatic:
MONTEVERDI, *L'Orfeo, Ahi, caso acerbo* (p. 76)
concerto:
VIVALDI, *Concerto Grosso*, Op. 3, No. 11 (p. 121)
BACH, *Brandenburg Concerto No. 2* (p. 190)
MOZART, *Piano Concerto in C* (p. 357)
concerto grosso:
VIVALDI, *Concerto Grosso*, Op. 3, No. 11 (p. 121)
BACH, *Brandenburg Concerto No. 2* (p. 190)
corrente (courante):
CORELLI, *Trio Sonata*, Op. 4, No. 1/II (p. 114)

da capo aria:
HANDEL, *Giulio Cesare, Piangerò* (p. 147)
duet, vocal:
MONTEVERDI, *Zefiro torna* (p. 79)
BACH, *Cantata No. 140/III, VI* (pp. 263, 278)
MOZART, *Don Giovanni, Là ci darem la mano* (p. 495)

French overture:
HANDEL, *Messiah*, Overture (p. 150)
frottola:
JOSQUIN, *Scaramella* (p. 31)
fugue:
BACH, *Organ Fugue in G minor* (p. 185)

gigue:
BACH, *Suite No. 3*, Gigue (p. 228)
ground bass (basso ostinato):
MONTEVERDI, *Zefiro torna* (p. 79)

PURCELL, *Dido and Aeneas, Dido's Lament* (p. 118)

harpsichord music:
SCARLATTI, *Sonata in C minor* (p. 289)

instrumental music:
CORELLI, *Trio Sonata,* Opus 4, No. 1 (p. 113)
VIVALDI, *Concerto Grosso in D minor,* Op. 3, No. 11 (p. 121)
HANDEL, *Messiah,* Overture (p. 150)
BACH, *Organ Fugue in G minor* (p. 185); *Brandenburg Concerto No. 2* (p. 190); *Suite No. 3* (p. 226)
SCARLATTI, *Sonata in C minor* (p. 289)
HAYDN, *Symphony No. 94* (p. 294)
MOZART, *Piano Concerto in C major* (p. 357); *Eine kleine Nachtmusik* (p. 451); *Symphony in G minor* (p. 500)
BEETHOVEN, *String Quartet,* Op. 18, No. 1 (p. 566); *Piano Sonata in C minor,* Op. 13 (p. 578); *Symphony No. 5* (p. 594)

introduction:
HANDEL, *Messiah,* Overture (p. 150)
HAYDN, *Symphony No. 94/I* (p. 294)
BEETHOVEN, *Piano Sonata,* Op. 13/I (p. 578)

Introit:
GREGORIAN CHANT, *Gaudeamus omnes* (p. 3)

keyboard music:
BACH, *Organ Fugue in G minor* (p. 185)
SCARLATTI, *Sonata in C minor* (p. 289)

BEETHOVEN, *Piano Sonata,* Op. 13 (p. 578)

Kyrie:
GREGORIAN CHANTS, *Kyrie XII* (p. 5); *Kyrie IV* (p. 7)
MACHAUT, *Messe de Notre Dame,* Kyrie (p. 7)

lament:
JOSQUIN, *Déploration sur la mort de Johan Okeghem* (p. 22)
PURCELL, *Dido and Aeneas, Dido's Lament* (p. 118)

madrigal:
ARCADELT, *Il bianco cigno* (p. 46)
MORLEY, *Sing We and Chant It* (p. 60)
WEELKES, *As Vesta Was Descending* (p. 89)

Mass movement:
GREGORIAN CHANTS, *Gaudeamus omnes* (p. 3); *Kyrie XII* (p. 5); *Kyrie IV* (p. 7); *Requiem aeternam* (p. 22)
MACHAUT, *Messe de Notre Dame,* Kyrie (p. 7)
JOSQUIN, *Missa L'homme armé,* Agnus Dei (p. 32)
PALESTRINA, *Missa Ascendo ad Patrem,* Sanctus (p. 49)

minuet and trio:
HAYDN, *Symphony No. 94/III* (p. 329)
MOZART, *Eine kleine Nachtmusik/III* (p. 464); *Symphony in G minor/III* (p. 539)

motet:
ANONYMOUS, *O miranda dei karitas—Salve mater salutifera—Kyrie* (p. 5)
DUFAY, *Alma redemptoris mater* (p. 12)

LASSUS, *Prophetiae sibyllarum* (p. 55)

GABRIELI, *Nunc dimittis* (p. 62)

operatic scene:
MONTEVERDI, *L'Orfeo* (p. 74)
PURCELL, *Dido and Aeneas* (p. 118)
HANDEL, *Giulio Cesare* (p. 147)
MOZART, *Don Giovanni* (p. 475)

oratorio:
HANDEL, *Messiah* (p. 150)

orchestral music:
VIVALDI, *Concerto Grosso in D minor*, Op. 3, No. 11 (p. 121)
HANDEL, *Messiah*, Overture (p. 150)
BACH, *Brandenburg Concerto No. 2* (p. 190); *Suite No. 3* (p. 226)
HAYDN, *Symphony No. 94* (p. 294)
MOZART, *Piano Concerto in C major* (p. 357); *Symphony in G minor* (p. 500)
BEETHOVEN, *Symphony No. 5* (p. 594)

organ music:
BACH, *Organ Fugue in G minor* (p. 185)

overture:
HANDEL, *Messiah*, Overture (p. 150)

passacaglia: *see* ground bass

piano music:
BEETHOVEN, *Piano Sonata*, Op. 13 (p. 578)

prelude:
CORELLI, *Trio Sonata*, Op. 4, No. 1/I (p. 113)

quartet, strings:
BEETHOVEN, *String Quartet*, Op. 18, No. 1 (p. 566)

quintet, strings:
MOZART, *Eine kleine Nachtmusik* (p. 451)

recitative:
MONTEVERDI, *L'Orfeo, Tu se' morta* (p. 74)
PURCELL, *Dido and Aeneas, Thy hand, Belinda!* (p. 118)
BACH, *Cantata No. 140/II*, V (pp. 262, 276)

rondo:
GLUCK, *Orfeo ed Euridice, Che farò senza Euridice?* (p. 291)
MOZART, *Piano Concerto in C/III* (p. 422)
HAYDN, *Symphony No. 94/IV* (p. 335)
BEETHOVEN, *Piano Sonata*, Op. 13/II, III (pp. 585, 588)

Sanctus:
PALESTRINA, *Missa Ascendo ad Patrem*, Sanctus (p. 49)

scherzo and trio:
BEETHOVEN, *Symphony No. 5/III* (p. 645)

slow introduction: *see* introduction

sonata:
CORELLI, *Trio Sonata*, Op. 4, No. 1 (p. 113)
SCARLATTI, *Sonata in C minor* (p. 289)
BEETHOVEN, *Piano Sonata*, Op. 13 (p. 578)

sonata-allegro form:
HAYDN, *Symphony No. 94/I* (p. 294)
MOZART, *Eine kleine Nachtmusik/I*, IV (pp. 451, 465); *Symphony in G minor/I*, II, IV (pp. 500, 526, 544)

BEETHOVEN, *Piano Sonata,* Op. 13/ I (578); *String Quartet,* Op. 18, No. 1/I (p. 566); *Symphony No. 5/I, IV* (pp. 594, 664)
sonata da camera:
  CORELLI, *Trio sonata,* Op. 4, No. 1 (p. 113)
sonata form: *see* sonata-allegro form
sonata-rondo form: *see* rondo form
song:
  BUSNOIS, *Amour nous traicte—Je m'en vois* (p. 18)
  JOSQUIN, *Scaramella* (p. 30)
  ANONYMOUS, *L'homme armé* (p. 32)
string quartet: *see* quartet
string quintet: *see* quintet
suite:
  BACH, *Suite No. 3* (p. 226)
symphony:
  HAYDN, *Symphony No. 94* (p. 294)
  MOZART, *Symphony in G minor* (p. 500)
  BEETHOVEN, *Symphony No. 5* (p. 594)

ternary form:
  BACH, *Cantata No. 140/VI* (p. 278)
  MOZART, *Eine kleine Nachtmusik/ II* (p. 459)
  see also: da capo aria; minuet and trio; scherzo and trio
theme and variations:
  HAYDN, *Symphony No. 94/II* (p. 317)
  BEETHOVEN, *Symphony No. 5/II* (p. 624)
  see also: ground bass
three-part form: *see* ternary form
trio, vocal:
  MOZART, *Don Giovanni,* Introduction (p. 478)
trio sonata:
  CORELLI, *Trio Sonata,* Op. 4, No. 1 (p. 113)
two-part form: *see* binary form

variations: *see* theme and variations; **ground bass**